COMMUNICATION & LANGUAGE IN EARLY CHILDHOOD TODAY

Sara Miller McCune founded Sage Publishing in 1965 to support the dissemination of useable knowledge and educate a global community. Sage publishes more than 1000 journals and over 800 new books each year, spanning a wide range of subject areas. Our growing selection of library products includes archives, data, case studies and video. Sage remains majority owned by our founder and after her lifetime will become owned by a charitable trust that secures the company's continued independence.

Los Angeles | London | New Delhi | Singapore | Washington DC | Melbourne

JULIE KENT
TANYA RICHARDSON

COMMUNICATION & LANGUAGE IN EARLY CHILDHOOD TODAY

1 Oliver's Yard
55 City Road
London EC1Y 1SP

2455 Teller Road
Thousand Oaks
California 91320

Unit No 323-333, Third Floor, F-Block
International Trade Tower Nehru Place
New Delhi 110 019
India

3 Church Street
#10-04 Samsung Hub
Singapore 049483

Library of Congress Control Number: 2024944302

British Library Cataloguing in Publication Data

A catalogue record for this book is available from the British Library

ISBN 978-1-5296-8977-8
ISBN 978-1-5296-8976-1 (pbk)

Editor: Amy Thornton
Development editor: Ruth Lily
Senior project editor: Chris Marke
Project management: TNQ Tech Pvt. Ltd.
Cover design: Wendy Scott
Typeset by: TNQ Tech Pvt. Ltd.
Printed and bound by CPI roup (UK) Ltd, Croydon, CR0 4YY

CONTENTS

ACKNOWLEDGEMENTS

We would like to express our thanks to everybody involved in the production of this book. The knowledge, practice examples and information that you have all shared is very much appreciated. You have all produced amazing chapters within short time frames whilst juggling the day jobs. We wouldn't have a book without you all.

Thank you.

Julie and Tanya

ABOUT THE EDITORS AND CONTRIBUTORS

About the editors

Dr Tanya Richardson is a Senior Lecturer in Early Years at the University of Northampton and is Programme Leader for the Early Childhood Studies programme. She has previously managed and led her own 'outstanding' day nursery and out of school club. The nursery setting was fortunate enough to have a forest school as part of its ethos and Tanya became very interested in the impact that this environment had on children's speech and language development. She therefore is lucky enough to have the practice wisdom that she is able to apply to the academic studies and her PhD researched the impact that different learning and play environments have on young children's speech and language development.

Julie Kent is a Senior Lecturer on the BA (Hons) Childhood degrees programmes and strand leader on the Education and Early Childhood MA programme at Nottingham Trent University. She initially qualified and practised as a Speech and Language Therapist in the National Health Service (NHS) for 15 years, working with children in school and community settings. Prior to working in higher education, Julie led the team in a Sure Start Children's Centre in rural Northamptonshire with a focus on developing the inter-agency working and the early communication support for children and families. Her current doctoral research interests are in the communication environment in Early Years settings and the interface between health and education in the support for children's early speech, language and communication development.

About the contributors

Bibiana Wigley is a qualified speech and language therapist who has worked across NHS, local authority teams and independent practice. Working in the East Midlands for 27 years, she has led teams to innovate and deliver accessible services in schools, early years settings and communities for children, families and the range of professionals that support them. Bibiana has lectured on both undergraduate and postgraduate courses for early years educators and SENCO and is passionate about the Early Years, promoting high quality professional development opportunities for the children's workforce with a particular interest in the use of coaching.

David McDonald works in public health in Nottingham. He has particular interests in supporting the well-being and health of people who are the most socially excluded and marginalised in society, and in working collaboratively with others as much as possible. He previously worked as a Speech and Language Therapist for around 15 years, specialising mostly in the early years.

Julia Harris is a speech and language therapist specialising in Early Years. She has extensive experience in training and coaching parents/carers and Early Years professionals to support children's communication skills. She has delivered and collaborated on several innovative speech and language projects within the NHS as part of skilling up the Early Years workforce.

Katarina Dolgan, MSc, is a senior consultant for primary teachers at the National Education Institute of Slovenia. Many of her recent activities are related to implementing and promoting outdoor learning in the Slovenian school system. By participating in a very successful international project for early language development in nature – ElaDiNa she gained international experiences and widened her horizons about outdoor learning in other European countries. Now she is trying to expand this knowledge among Slovenian primary teachers through different events, such as seminars, conferences, study sessions, publishing a magazine with articles about outdoor learning, etc.

Laura Sanders holds an MA in Early Childhood and Education (Integrated working with children and families), holds Early Years Teacher Status, a BA Degree and further Early Years qualifications such as infant massage and baby signing. Laura has been a Sessional Lecturer in Further Education in a college and Higher Education in a university. She supported the creation of a new BA degree and has been the lead moderator since 2021. Laura is the proprietor and Director of two Early Years Settings since 2012 in the East Midlands as well as being a mother to two boys aged 9 and 13.

Michelle Bugby is a Senior Lecturer at the University of Northampton and an Early Years Teacher with extensive experience in managing and leading Early Years practice. Her research focuses on young children's reading behaviours, motivations and attitudes, the home literacy environment, children's rights and participation and creative and visual methodologies. She is dedicated to advancing the field of Early Childhood Education through innovative research and practical application, aiming to enhance educational practices and children's learning experiences.

Nyree Nicholson is the Programme Leader for Foundation Degrees and BA (Hons) top programmes in Education, Early Childhood and Childhood, Youth and Families at Bishop Grosseteste University in Lincoln, UK. Her research focuses on supporting early speech, language and communication needs, collaborative practice and the professionalism of the early years sector. Nyree's academic journey began as a childminder and foster carer, leading her to earn a Foundation Degree, BA, MA and PhD in related fields. She is dedicated to evaluating normative development within early years education, advocating for educational equity and addressing the complexities faced by children with diverse backgrounds, including those with Special Educational Needs and Disabilities (SEND).

Rachael Webster is a Lecturer in the Institute of Education at Nottingham Trent University, teaching modules in the fields of Special and Inclusive Education, Early Years care and education and educational leadership and management across undergraduate professional and academic courses. She is also involved in community and industry partnership projects to promote diversity and inclusion, as well-being a qualified advisory teacher specialising in multiple disabilities and sensory impairments. Rachael was a teacher for many years in specialist SEND settings working with learners who have complex needs and multiple disabilities in schools in Leicester and Coventry.

Sue Hobson is an Early Years Consultant. She is an experienced Early Years teacher who has worked in Tower Hamlets, London and in Leicester. She worked for 13 years with Leicester City's Early Years Support Team teaching and supporting children from birth to 5 with additional needs and their families. She has a particular interest in special needs, English as an additional language, family learning and the impact that trauma has on the attachment, behaviour and emotional well-being of our youngest children. She is an enthusiastic and creative trainer who enjoys the challenge of making learning accessible and enjoyable to a varied audience. She is a mother of five and grandmother of 15 and lives in Leicester with her husband, Pete.

FOREWORD

The Editors, Julie Kent and Tanya Richardson, have assembled contributions from academics, speech and language therapists and early year professionals, to address how best to support speech, language and communication (SLC) in early childhood. This is a timely and much needed contribution to the field given that many global reports continue to highlight (i) the ongoing struggle to support children's SLC need in the early years, (ii) the difficulty in closing gaps later in childhood and (iii) the poorer, longer-term outcomes reported for many children with early SLC difficulties. There is no doubt that quality early years support is critical for all children, but especially so for those having trouble communicating. Early years professionals play a fundamental role in identifying children who may be having trouble communicating, and therefore the book's focus is on positive ways in which early years professionals can support children's SLC needs by working constructively and in partnership with families, early year staff and a range of professionals.

The book is written primarily for students of early childhood studies; however, it will have broader appeal for all health and education students interested in early childhood. Many of the chapters draw on the author's primary research and the format of each chapter encourages critical thinking throughout, with the use of boxes that contain reflections and case studies followed by questions for the reader. Each chapter opens with a list of critical points and ends with a list of critical questions and a list of resources and further reading.

In the opening chapter the Editors emphasise the importance of early SLC development in forming the foundation for later learning as well as the leadership that is required in this important space. The first set of chapters cover a fascinating and important list of topics including total communication approaches, navigating the digital landscape, the impact of outdoor pedagogy on children's communication and an overview of approaches to supporting language development within natural environments. This included discussion of forest schools in the United Kingdom and a comparison of case studies from a project undertaken across Slovenia, Germany and Sweden. The middle chapters focus on how to develop the requisite skills to work effectively with parents including an examination of relevant research, consideration of a systems perspective and an overview of the components of a supportive early year's framework. One of the chapters describes an intergenerational approach and incorporates a case study to illustrate the benefits of intergenerational play on SLC development and another considers what a successful multilingual and multicultural early years learning community might look like. The final chapters challenge the reader to go beyond interdisciplinary and inter-agency collaboration to develop multiagency approaches and include an overview of the evolution of multiagency working focusing primarily on speech and language therapy services. This thread continued in the next chapter in a discussion about how early years professionals might be better supported to develop children's SLC skills, strategies that might facilitate better support and multiagency approaches and examples of such initiatives in the United Kingdom.

Throughout the book the need for a consistent, whole of setting, multiagency approach is advocated that recognises the uniqueness of each child and family. In the final chapter the editors reflect on the past challenges faced by early years professionals and do not shy away from outlining some of the future challenges faced in supporting children's SLC needs in the early years and the complexity in doing so. As is encouraged throughout the book, the Editors urge the reader to reflect on their experiences and practice and in assembling this book have provided readers with some of the support they might need to challenge practice. Their advice '...to stay curious and be creative...' is welcome and relevant.

Sheena Reilly AM
FASSA FAHMS FSPA FRCSLT
Emeritus Professor
Health Group
Griffith University, Queensland, Australia

INTRODUCTION: WHAT DO WE UNDERSTAND BY SPEECH, LANGUAGE AND COMMUNICATION AND UNIVERSAL GOOD PRACTICE?

THIS CHAPTER

By actively reading this chapter and engaging with the material, you will be able to:

- Consider the theoretical developmental perspectives around children's speech and language development.
- Explore how different approaches to working in this area can enhance understanding of communication practice in a wider context beyond the setting.
- Consider practical examples of how children can be supported and development can be enhanced.
- Have an understanding of the structure of the book and the chapters that follow.

Introduction

This chapter will explore, discuss and support good practice in relation to children's speech, language and communication (SLC). The text is intended to support students on a range of undergraduate courses, including Childhood and Early Childhood degrees as well as students progressing to postgraduate study in related areas. However, it will also be of interest to students studying specific child development modules on Psychology, Speech and Language Therapy and Linguistics courses.

When we consider what we mean by good practice within this area, we firstly need to understand how children develop with regards to their SLC. There are many different viewpoints on how this happens and how children can learn so much in such a short space of time. This chapter will look at various theories around how this happens, but whatever your viewpoint or stance on this, there is no doubting that young children learn language rapidly. Saxton (2017, p. 8) reports that once a child has mastered their first word, then initially new words appear at 'a gentle rate' of around one word per week. Tamis-LeMonda et al. (2001) state that when the repertoire reaches around 50 words, this rate of acquisition increases significantly and increases by one or two per day, with as many as 10 new words a day being added to the child's repertoire (Clark, 1993). This means that by the time a child reaches the age of six, this will result in a vocabulary of between 10,000 (Bloom and Markson, 1998) and 14,000 words (Clark, 1993). This is a huge achievement, and as we explore this further in the chapter that follows and subsequent chapters, we will begin to consider how, as professionals, we can support this achievement accordingly.

What is speech, language and communication?

As practitioners, it is important to be mindful that communication is not just spoken language. Developmental psycholinguistics focuses on language acquisition and the processes which enable children to become proficient in the use of language. This field of study explores a number of crucial skills which underpin children's development of spoken language or 'talk' and covers the way in which children learn to perceive, attend to, understand, produce words and use them to communicate (Sudrajat, 2017). Trevarthen's detailed parent–infant communication research since the 1970s confirms how language acquisition emerges from the context of non-verbal communication through early shared interactions (Trevarthen in Bullowa, 1978).

Children's speech and language is supported by a number of other skills, and communication is a multifaceted skill (Morgan and Dipper, 2018). A useful representation of the representing the interconnectedness of the network of skills which come together in different ways in each child is that of Charatan's 2006 target profile diagram (see Figure 1). This model provides a nuanced picture to show the network of social, cognitive and physical skills which combine to underpin communication development.

How does SLC develop?

Historically, there has been a debate between theoretical developmental perspectives which are influenced by the beliefs held about how children acquire spoken language. Students are encouraged to find out much more about this in other dedicated texts, and this chapter will not revisit the history of the nature/nurture debate which revolves around the nativist view of language development being the result of biologically driven capacities as opposed to social learning theories which suggest that language is learned through exposure to, and imitation of, the spoken word. Chomsky (1957) first proposed that language learning is innate and determined by natural, inbuilt and specific brain structures and language acquisition functions. This view challenged existing perspectives which suggested that children can only language in a mechanistic way by imitating the language which they are

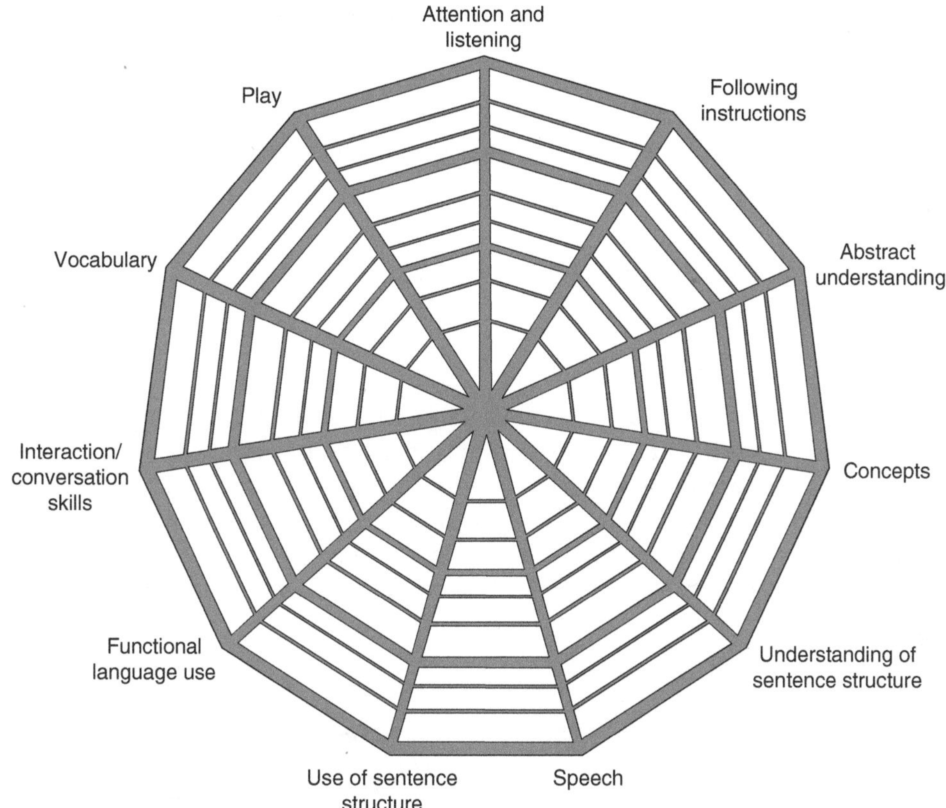

Figure 1 Example of target profile diagram (Charatan, 2006)

exposed to and that they continue to produce utterances which are reinforced by the responses of caregivers; this is seen in the views of theorists such as Skinner (1957). Other social constructivists, such as Vygotsky (1978), make the connection between the social context in which language occurs and the way in which shared meanings in relationships are initially communicated through sounds, words and feelings and are gradually refined into shared language patterns. It is evident, however, that children are born with a desire for connection and to communicate, and that even their earliest actions are intentionally communicative, not random and designed to maintain communication relationships with caregivers from the start (Murray and Andrews, 2005).

Even considering this, how is it that children learn complex skills in both understanding and manipulating language with very little life experience and also with differing life experiences? Although children's early speech and communication appears to follow generally recognisable stages and patterns, there are individual differences in language acquisition. Children's early language is often not a direct imitation of the words and sounds which they hear. It is important to recognise and challenge assumptions that children in all cultures and communities learn language in similar ways (Rowland, 2013). Current theoretical perspectives in this fascinating sphere are driven by debates and explorations of how biology and experience operate together in communication and language (C&L) development with the belief that there is an interplay between biology and environment where newborns apply innate social and attentional preferences which equip them to learn from their social environment (ibid). These perspectives imply that children are born prepared for communication as a basis for safety and survival.

Money's framework of means, reasons and opportunities (1997) provides a useful structure through which to explore children's early communication and possible barriers to good communication development.

Means

This relates to 'how' children communicate and is based initially in nature or the child's innate communicative abilities, including their cognitive, auditory and motor skills. Communication may be verbal, using noises, cries and words, or non-verbal, for example, through facial expression, gestures, pointing and other physical postures or movements. Practitioners should be familiar with children's preferred means of communication and respond to all attempts to communicate.

Reasons

This relates to 'why' children communicate. Children may have many reasons to communicate, ranging from basic comfort needs such as hunger or discomfort, through expressing specific intentions to wanting to make a social relationship and have a 'chat'! It is in this area where adults as communication partners can have a significant influence on the child's continuing communication development through being attuned to the child's attempts to communicate.

Opportunities

This is where the social element of language acquisition can be seen. Children need opportunities to communicate with others. The presence of a responsive adult who provides good communication environments, gives time to allow a child to initiate an interaction, allows genuine choices and shows interest in the child's activity can support this element of the process.

The following short case study exemplifies some of these elements considered essential for good communication.

CASE STUDY 0.1 BABY EZRA

Ezra aged 11 months is sitting at his dad's feet and trying to attract his attention.

He pulls himself up on his dad's legs and vocalises 'uh' loudly, tugging on his dad's trousers.

His dad looks down and smiles, holding out his arms and says: 'do you want to come up?'

Ezra looks up and holds his own arms out.

His dad bends down and lifts him onto his lap saying 'Up you come. UP!'

This routine is repeated several times with lots of smiles with Ezra being lifted up, put down and vocalising before being picked up again.

REFLECTION 0.1

- *What does this exchange show you about Ezra's means of communication, intention or reason to communicate and opportunity to use his words alongside his non-verbal skills?*
- *What do you notice about the adult's language in this interaction?*
- *How will you use Birth to 5 Matters (Early Education, 2021) which states that 'listening to children's voices and recognising that these are expressed in a range of ways, including non-verbally, is central to inclusive practice' (np online)?*

Social context for language learning

From the knowledge that we have about early attachment and relationships, it is possible to see how communication interactions occur from birth. The works of Trevarthen (1978) and Brazelton et al. (1975) have been revelatory in the Early Years. Their prolific research has explored aspects of reciprocity in parent–child interactions and identified the centrality of a contingent adult response to the child in supporting early shared understanding and communicative intent over many years. These perspectives show how attachment supports child agency and autonomy as part of the communication relationship. Murray and Egan (2014) note the quality and quantity of spoken language that children hear from care-givers in their Early Years is an important influence on language development, and Beuker et al. (2013) explore the importance of shared attention in the development of early SLC.

Considering the insights which can be taken from a range of developmental or learning theories, it is evident that children do, to some extent, imitate, use and build on the language which they are exposed to in their own communication.

There is a view that children from lower socio-economic (SE) groups are exposed to language environments which are less rich, and therefore, their own communication and language development can be impoverished (Hart and Risley, 1995). Critiques of this perspective challenge these social stereotypes and prejudices, pointing to the need not to judge non-standard language patterns as well as to recognize additional contextual factors for some families. It is crucial to recognise the possibility that impoverished language environments may occur across all social classes for a number of different reasons, including as a result of the debated area of child and parent screen use (Mustonen et al., 2022). However, this SE perspective, despite being highly contested, has become part of the mainstream view, for example, in education and has been the basis of a number of initiatives in the Early Years in the United Kingdom, for example, the Surestart programme (Eisenstadt date), the First 1,001 Days movement, targeted Local Authority Early Intervention programmes and the recent Family Hubs initiative.

Note about universal good practice

In the light of our understanding of the way in which children's communication and language skills develop in a social context, it is vital to recognise the significance of the levels of confidence and competence in Early Years practitioners in providing a good communication environment in a nursery setting. Dame Tickell in her review of the Early Years Foundation Stage (EYFS) (2011) emphasised that it is essential the Early Years workforce has the necessary skills to support and develop communication as 'within the first years of the child's life, children have laid the groundwork to becoming proficient in language which is the core of communication' (p. 94). Leadership of the setting should set the tone for good communication practice between staff as well as with children (Hobson and Farley in Kent and Moran, 2019). Coughlin and Baird (2013) reflect on how pedagogical leaders will model what works for children with the adults in the settings. So, as leaders of good practice in communication with children, adults in an Early Years setting should develop their critical thinking in examining their practice and its impact on setting-wide communication relationships. Taking a curious approach to your own learning and development, reflecting on what works and modelling this, creates a culture of openness and professional enquiry which can lead to stronger communication relationships and a deeper awareness of what might be the barriers for your children and families.

The context

If the above is what we know about how speech and language develops, then what do we do in practice to mirror this? The section that follows will consider this question from the multifaceted contexts of education, health and social care. It is recognised that this holistic approach to children and their development is critical when compiling a full picture of the child and their family.

The educational context

When considering early childhood education and care, it is recognised that there are multiple elements to take into account to ensure children's speech and language development is not just supported but enhanced. It is widely documented that young children need high-quality, effective interactions (Fisher, 2016). When considering what constitutes an 'effective' interaction, Fisher (2016) reports that the Oxfordshire Adult-Child Interaction Project (2014) asks you to consider the following question:

> *Did the child gain something positive from this interaction that s/he would not otherwise have had?*

It could be said that this stance should be applied to all aspects of education. Without becoming too political, there is much going on within the educational landscape at the time of writing that does not consider whether the child is able to 'gain something positive from the interaction'. Take school readiness for example. In a recent survey by KindredSquared, it was found that 91% of parents felt that their child was ready for school, but in stark contrast, teachers reported that 35% of children were not ready by their standards for reception classes (KindredSquared, 2024). When looking at this from a speech and language perspective, the study found that 30% of children, when starting reception, are unable to communicate their needs, 37% do not know how to listen or respond to basic instructions and 25% do not have basic language skills (i.e. able to say name or answer basic questions). This mismatch of teacher perception and parent perception is obviously concerning and leads us to consider how the government agenda is working alongside the family agenda.

REFLECTION 0.2

Read the report from KindredSquared (discussed above) to find out more details about perceptions of school readiness, focusing particularly on the areas relating to speech and language.

- *Considering the stark contrast between teachers' perceptions and parents' perceptions in this report, how could you help in this area when working within an Early Years context?*
- *What could you do as a professional to aid in this area?*

Also, when we look through the educational lens and how we support children's speech and language, we tend to see that there appears to be a strong correlation portrayed between speech and language and the influence of literacy. Resources that are made available to support speech and language are often equated with literacy and hence with phonics. When we consider the statistics highlighted above, outlining how many children are struggling with basic communication skills, then literacy and phonics seems a big ask in this context. How can a child sound out letters and attempt to form words when they are not able to create the speech sounds needed to do so? The focus of this book therefore is intended to move away from the narrow focus of literacy and phonics-related concepts and instead to consider SLC in practice from a holistic and relational perspective.

The health context

Speech and language, as was mentioned earlier in this chapter, is partly biological in the way that it develops. The physical, as well as the cognitive effort required in speech and language, when you stop to think about it, is immense.

REFLECTION 0.3

Start to say some phonics sounds.

As you say these, consider what parts of your mouth and voice box are doing the work.

Be really conscious of what your lips are doing, where your tongue is in your mouth, how the sound is being generated.

Now think about what impact there would be if one of these parts of your physicality was not working properly. Bear in mind that you probably have not considered your palate function or whether sound is voiced or voiceless!

By undertaking the reflection above this will hopefully have made you think about how physically complex forming the spoken word can be. And then there is obviously the art of listening and the cognitive function required to process what is heard and to formulate a response. So if one part of the communication chain is not working as it should, then this could require intervention, and this could be where the speech and language therapy (SALT) team assist. But what can be done within practice to support this alongside the SALT team? The case study below, from Jo Hutchinson, Head of School Effectiveness for North Northamptonshire Council, England, outlines a successful project that has been happening within her local authority to do just this.

CASE STUDY 0.2 THE START WELL PROJECT

The Start Well project was created with the purpose of developing partnerships and facilitating continuous improvement across a group of Early Years education settings and providers. This small-scale research study took place in a locality area where the Good Level of Development (GLD) was significantly lower than national average. Initial evidence gathered from participants unsurprisingly identified that speech and language was one of the main concerns and had worsened since the COVID-19 pandemic.

Consequently, a research project was launched in partnership with the University of Northampton (UON). The brief was to explore how indoor and outdoor play and learning spaces impact on young children's communication and language development.

Participants made several changes to their environments, including improving access to quality books, enabling provocations through the introduction of old phones/cameras, increasing exposure to the natural world encompassing wildlife, with greater exposure to music.

Early indications show that these environmental developments have improved children's speech and language. In all settings, the excitement and engagement has prompted an increase in the confidence of children, triggering their use of a much broader range of vocabulary. Practitioners commented: 'this project has really made a difference', with others noting 'children's imagination has been developed further, this is benefitting the speech and language'.

As discussed above, in addition to the biological requirements of speech and language, there are also the considerations around nurture – the way that the environment and those within it support the child's development. When thinking of this from a health perspective, one recent event that springs to mind is the impact of COVID-19. It is widely documented that the pandemic deprived children of social skills. The Education Endowment Foundation (EEF) research (2022) suggested that the measures taken to combat the pandemic have deprived the youngest children of social contact and experiences essential for increasing vocabulary. Less or no contact with grandparents, social distancing, no play dates and the wearing of face coverings in public have left children less exposed to conversations and everyday experiences. ICAN (2023) states that 'in order to meet the needs of children and young people, it's important that health, education and third sector providers work together at the local level to support an integrated approach. The aim of any investment in new initiatives would be to enhance and add value and capacity to support existing provision, not to replace them. Covid has created more need for support, not less – we should be adding more support for children now, not taking it away'.

REFLECTION 0.4

Jo Hutchinson highlighted in her case study above how North Northamptonshire Council identified an issue with speech and language development and put measures in place to bring about change. She talks about how the local authority

(Continued)

(Continued)

worked with settings, practitioners and a local university to join up research and practice with the aim of improving outcomes for children.

Is there anything happening within the area in which you are studying or working in that shows joined up working in any way?

It may be worthwhile exploring what is happening in your locality, if anything, that involves professionals working together.

Ask around and see what is happening.

If you can't find anything, it might be something that you could write to your Local Authority and suggest?

The social care context

When thinking about the social care context of early childhood, speech and language may not be the first thing that spring to mind. You may think that social workers and other professionals who work in this crucial area do not really have much to do with this area of young children's development. Professor Eunice Lumsden, a registered social worker and advocate for children, explains below how her work as a social worker has been shaped by her awareness of the impact that adverse childhood experiences can have on speech and language development.

CASE STUDY 0.3 PROFESSOR LUMSDEN

In this case study, Professor Lumsden discusses how the experiences that young children have impact on speech and language but also in the ways that they communicate.

> One of the most valuable lessons that the children, young people and adults, taught me as a social worker was the importance of speech and language development in Early Childhood. Their earliest experiences of trauma, abuse and moves in and out of the care system meant they had gaps in their language, limited vocabulary and were unable to communicate their needs verbally. Many struggled in education settings, with their earliest experiences acting as barriers to educational achievement.
>
> I was often involved in situations where those who were unable to express themselves verbally, communicated through what was deemed to be challenging behaviour. For some, this resulted in school exclusion, moving

from their foster home or, if they had been adopted, returning to the care system. These experiences have been my drivers to improve support for families and training for all those working in early childhood and beyond, to understand the importance of holistic child development and how the building blocks for speech and language development begin at the start of life.

The above case study shows that children do not always use formal language to communicate their emotions and desires, and Chapter 2 will consider this further, in greater depth. In the meantime, consider the reflective questions below to apply the case study to your practice and think about how the issues raised will impact your work with children.

REFLECTION 0.5

- *What ways might children communicate their feelings, likes and dislikes through non-verbal methods?*
- *How could you respond to these methods of communication in a positive way?*
- *How could you educate your peers to see this means of communication as something more than challenging behaviour?*
- *Who could you seek support from to aid you further in this area?*

Inclusive and holistic practice

Although the above has discussed the three areas of child services as three distinct areas, the reality is often that these cross over and what works best is when these three services work together, holistically, with the child and the family at the centre of the process. If a child needs additional support, then one of these particular services may be drawn upon more than the others, and this will be dependent on the individual circumstances of the context in which that child is situated. There is not a 'one-size-fits-all' approach to supporting children and whatever lens you view children's support through – be it education, health or social care – it is important to remember the uniqueness of each child and their family circumstances. As you therefore progress through this book, this is important to keep in mind. Each child, and their circumstances, is different, and our practice should reflect this accordingly.

How the chapters will contribute

Although the authors throughout this book will refer to the current practice framework in England, the text also includes examples from global practice and elements which have possibilities for a wider implementation beyond the Early Years Foundation Stage (EYFS) (DfE, 2024). It will engage with a broad and comprehensive perspective on C&L which looks beyond a single prime area of child development to encompass the significance of communication as relational and based in beliefs about child agency and voice.

The book employs a systems perspective with chapters exploring the elements in Bronfenbrenner's ecological systems theory (1977), beginning in the microsystem with children's closest communication relationships, moving through the mesosystem where settings work together with families, other professionals and within their community, examining policy, provision and practice from wider exosystem perspectives and challenging the wider culture and changing systems around ways of working to support children's SLC.

In Chapter 1, Julie Kent considers children's C&L and what practitioners bring to their practice in supporting this area of children's learning and development. The chapter explores the centrality of having a strong knowledge of children's communication development and provides challenge to practitioners to move beyond a surface engagement with their existing knowledge.

With an increasing number of Early Years children entering school with below-age-related communication skills, inclusive approaches are becoming increasingly common in our Early Years settings. In Chapter 2, Rachael Webster discusses the evidence base for current practice and outlines some underpinning theories and actions of total communication in Early Years practice.

Chapter 3 considers another specific aspect of the communication environment: the technology which is available to children and settings. Michelle Bugby explores this sometimes-contested area and discuss the impact of technology on SLC. This chapter looks at the benefits of the use of technology as well as the barriers to the use of technological tools. This chapter gives practical ideas of how this can be supported in practice and also how practitioners can work with parents to support in this area.

In Chapter 4, in an area which can be seen as in complete contrast to the application of ICT, Tanya Richardson explores the impact of nature and the outdoors on communication and language development. This is a topic that is very rarely discussed in literature so will provide a useful addition to the narrative around SLC. The chapter explores what elements within a natural environment prompt language learning and vocabulary with some practical examples.

Chapter 5 will provide an international slant on the use of the outdoors to support children's speech and language development. Tanya Richardson and Katarina

Dolgan use case studies from Germany, Sweden, Slovenia and England to compare and contrast practice across these European countries with examples of what works well within natural spaces.

Using evidence from a small-scale piece of research undertaken in a community Early Years setting, Chapter 6 will consider what works in supporting parents with their children's developing SLC, particularly in relation to how possible early needs are identified and supported. In Early Years (EY) practice, there is a space where child-sensitive communication approaches in the home and good practice in settings can have an early impact on children's skills in this area of development, preventing later delays and associated disadvantage.

In Chapter 7, Laura Sanders provides a very personal insight into the development of an intergenerational project in her community from a setting manager perspective. The journey of this project demonstrates the value of intergenerational approaches in the Early Years and their impact on children's communication.

Chapter 8 supports the consideration of communication with children with English as an additional language (EAL) through the lens of good practice and practitioner experiences in some specific communities. This chapter, written by Sue Hobson, a practitioner, advisor and consultant with many years' experience in Leicester and inner London communities, challenges practitioners to move beyond general good practice guidance to view their practice with children and families through a critical lens.

Chapter 9 considers the evolution of multiagency approaches in early childhood Speech and Language Services, tracing the growth and development of services over the decades. Using a collection of case studies sourced from doctoral research that illuminates the experiences of practitioners in various regions, Nyree Nicholson provides a comparative analysis of multiagency efforts at the national level versus more localised initiatives and a discussion on the variation of support available across different geographical locations.

Building on the practitioner vignettes and discussion of local multiagency initiatives in Chapter 9, SLTs from the Notts Early Years team will use chapter 10 to outline ways in which speech and language therapists can work collaboratively with Early Years practitioners to support all children's SLC development. The chapter explores how training, coaching and the development of local communities of practice can form part of successful evidence-informed approaches including the Coaching Early Conversations Interactions and Language (CECIL) project and place them in the context of current Government guidance and initiatives.

In the final chapter, Julie Kent and Tanya Richardson identify the main 'take aways' from the preceding chapters and consolidate these into final challenges to, and reflections on, communication practice in the Early Years and the surrounding system.

1 LEADERSHIP OF COMMUNICATION AND LANGUAGE

JULIE KENT

THIS CHAPTER

By actively reading this chapter and engaging with the material, you will be able to:

- Recognise that children's communication and language (C&L) development underpins aspects of later life outcomes.
- Consider the importance of maintaining strong professional knowledge of children's learning and development in the area of C&L.
- Recognise the knowledge and skills which Early Years practitioners (EYPs) should hold in this area.
- View yourself as part of the wider system of good communication practice with children and within teams.
- Challenge aspects of the communication practice within your setting and team and explore creative ways to support members of the team with their continuing professional development in the area of C&L.
- Begin to reflect on the issues which may be encountered around children's additional speech, language and communication needs (SLCN).

Introduction

As discussed in the introduction chapter, children's C&L is arguably one of the most fundamental areas of learning and development. Children's early speech, language and communication (SLC) is viewed as an essential area of children's learning and development among Early Years theorists, for example, Vygotsky (1978), who viewed the role of language as being central to a child's cognitive development. There is a growing consensus on the centrality of language to children's early learning and development along with a recognition of the importance of early intervention where delays and difficulties in SLC exist (Ofsted, 2016).

This really matters for practice in early childhood, particularly in the climate of concerns about the school readiness of children, the influence of SLC on that and the emphasis on the role of early intervention in supporting children with SLCN (Ofsted, 2016). It is crucial to recognise that some of the context around children's early SLC is driven by the school readiness agenda, that is, the child's developmental readiness to access the learning opportunities available when they enter the reception year (YR). This chapter uses some familiar practice frameworks to explore these issues and support practitioners to develop confidence in leading in this crucial area.

The UK national context

The recent YouGov school readiness survey (2024) identified in the introduction contrasts the views of parents with the views of reception teachers in relation to meeting milestones across a number of developmental areas, including physical, self-care, social skills, attention and listening, understanding and following simple instructions and basic written and verbal skills. The report places particular emphasis on the additional demands on teaching resources to support children in these key developmental areas. In relation to C&L, 56% of schools have needed to dedicate more time and resources to improving children's early language skills, including investing in staff training to develop expertise in this key area. The report emphasises the fact that gaps at this stage are very hard to close and that there are long-term implications for children who are falling behind at this point. The finding that teachers suggest the quality and availability of good EY provision in supporting children's learning and development is a key element which provides a considerable challenge to those working in the field.

This view is echoed in practice; in the Early Years Foundation Stage (EYFS) framework for England (DfE, 2024), C&L is a prime area, and children's spoken language is described as 'the area of development ...(which) underpins all seven areas of learning and development' (p. 9). The focus in the EYFS is on the day-to-day practice of EYPs in providing opportunities through a 'language-rich environment' (p. 9) for children to interact and build their spoken language skills. It is acknowledged widely in practice guidance and research that the quality of early communication environments and interactions, particularly in childcare provisions, underpins children's developmental progress in this key area (Stewart and Waldfogel, 2017). However, it is also important to recognise that communication is more than just spoken interaction. For example, in Ireland, practitioners are guided by the Aistear early childhood curriculum framework (NCCA, 2009) which has 'communicating' as one of its four key themes. This practice framework has a focus which goes beyond children's spoken language to encompass the many verbal and non-verbal ways in which children communicate and continually identifies the centrality of the communication partnership between the adult and the child from 0 to 6. The Welsh Government also takes a wide and holistic view of children's SLC. In its Early Years SLC delivery plan, 'Talk with me', (Welsh Government, 2020) it states 'speech, language and communication (SLC) skills are essential for children's positive health, well-being, education and future employment outcomes' (p. 5). Here, there is a perspective which looks beyond the early years of a child's life, viewing the communication foundations which are built in these years as foundational to future long-term outcomes for the developing child and throughout their lifespan.

This perspective is taken even further in the ethos underpinning Scotland's EY framework (Scottish Government, 2009) where there is a strong emphasis on the impact of early learning experiences on long-term outcomes resulting in a move away from focusing on individual area of learning and development. The Scottish approach takes a system-wide perspective which looks at C&L as part of the child's holistic long-term development rather than an isolated area of learning. The influence of the EY is viewed beyond a preparation for school, as the basis for 'the pattern for our future adult life' EY, later life and the success of Scottish society. Here, children's holistic development across all areas inextricably connected to parental outcomes in health, employment and well-being.

This perspective is also recognised by researchers in child development and health who have made clear links between delays in children's C&L development, social disadvantage, educational attainment and long-term life chances (Law et al., 2017). This research has been foundational to many of the early intervention programmes which we may be familiar with, such as the Surestart programme, Family Hubs and other local Early Help programmes within areas defined as being disadvantaged. An example of this is the Small Steps, Big Changes programme in Nottingham, England. An evaluation of this programme explored how parents were supported to engage in specific C&L supporting activities with their children, in particular, shared reading for pleasure to support greater shared communication in the long term (Tura et al., 2020).

REFLECTION 1.1

The Scottish EY framework highlights the need for EY practice to revolve around 'breaking cycles of poverty, inequality and poor outcomes in and through early years' (p. 3), while Law et al.'s research (2017) makes associations between children's early communication needs and long-term disadvantage.

- *What do you think this might mean for your own practice and leadership of communication practice in the setting?*

C&L as an area of developmental concern

The Scottish policy focus reflects a longstanding and growing concern about the ways in which children's' early C&L has an influence well into later life. This perspective has also been at the heart of work over a number of years outside of educational frameworks, for example, within the health service (PHE, 2020), speech and language therapy services and wider children's services. Because of its significance beyond developmental attainment, C&L is also the area of children's development which is often of greatest concern in an Early Years (EY) context where children with speech, language and communication needs (SLCN) of many types are identified for the first time. Early identification and intervention are considered essential to later development in both the short and long term (Nicholson, 2021). As stated above, research has increased the recognition of the role that early SLC difficulties can play in a child's long-term life chances (Beard, 2018) and has highlighted how delays in children's early language and literacy can go on to be linked to long-term educational, health, well-being and employment outcomes. As a consequence, this can result in a sense of additional responsibility as well as providing an impetus to ensuring high-quality provision by practitioners when working to support children's SLC. In his 2018 review of provision for children with SLCN, Bercow stated that an 'understanding of speech, language and communication should be embedded in initial qualifications and continuing professional development for all relevant practitioners' (p. 3). Policy expectations, practice guidance and interagency professional frameworks all espouse the importance of children's earliest relationships, particularly as they relate to C&L development (PHE, 2020), and there is a growing recognition of the centrality of children's C&L to their social, emotional and learning outcomes.

Research by the Sutton Trust over a number of years has also contributed to building an evidence base which shows how delays in children's early SLC skills are a key factor in ongoing social disadvantage and poorer life chances (Sutton Trust, 2024), making the significant connection between educational and health outcomes and placing children's SLC firmly as a public health concern not just an educational one. The longitudinal Effective Provision of Pre-school Education (EPPE) (Sylva et al., 2004) and Study of Early Education and Development (SEED) projects (DfE, 2021) have made similar connections between SLC needs and later life outcomes with particular emphasis on the importance of the need for practitioners in the Early Years to have a sound knowledge of children's development and a good grasp of appropriate pedagogical approaches. In fact, the SEED study emphasises the positive impact of good quality education on children's verbal abilities for all children but particularly those from the most disadvantaged backgrounds. The need for workforce development has been a theme across much valuable and well-regarded research data from both education and health, with a recognition of the need for a highly skilled workforce committed to continuing professional development and integrated working across child and family services.

The knowledge and skills of the EY workforce

UK Early Years frameworks and research studies promote a perspective on communication as a two-way process, highlighting that it is crucial to recognise the central role of the EY practitioner here as, along with their parents/carers, they interact with the child the most. As far back as 2011, Dame Tickell in her review of the EYFS (2011) emphasised that it is essential the Early Years workforce has the necessary skills to support and develop communication as 'within the first years of the child's life, children have laid the groundwork to becoming proficient in language which is the core of communication' (p. 94). This was further echoed the following year in the Nutbrown review of early education and childcare qualifications (2012) and has been reiterated many times since, including in Ofsted's 2023 review of the impacts of high-quality Early Years education on children's future well-being. As was discussed earlier in this chapter, children's C&L is identified as being central to the agenda around impacts and future attainment.

This emphasis can feel daunting for practitioners who may not feel confident in their knowledge and skills in this area, and a number of pieces of research have surveyed EYPs to investigate their levels of confidence and training in this area. Mcleod (2011) explores EYPs' ownership of language and communication skills and concluded that EYPs may not be fully confident in the underpinning pedagogical approaches which support good communication practice, hinting at disparities in training and practice across the EY sector. However, Blackburn and Aubrey (2016) found that although EYPs may not have had specific training in C&L, they expressed confidence about their day-to-day practice in identifying and supporting children's communication needs. Brebner et al. (2016) interviewed EYPs and found they expressed a strong understanding of children's early communication development and related this to their close relationships working with the children and families in their care. This research demonstrates that a well-trained practitioner who has daily close interactions with the children in their care is in a strong position to provide insights into children's communication development and can support this prime area of learning through well-informed pedagogy and practice.

It is important to recognise the knowledge and skills of the EY practitioner and what they bring to the expertise in the field of children's C&L. As key professionals in the field of children, childhood, development and learning, we can draw on some of the fundamentals of practice in considering leadership and working together in this prime area. In early childhood in the United Kingdom, many children attend formal education settings from increasingly younger ages as result of funded places. The interactions that those children have with Early Years educators (EYEs) will have an impact on their C&L skills (Pinto et al., 2013). The following case study explores a practitioner's perspectives on their knowledge and skills in supporting children's C&L.

CASE STUDY 1.1 PRACTITIONER INSIGHTS

This EYP was interviewed and spoke about the way in which the team has a whole-setting approach to supporting children's early SLC. She reflects particularly on how the team uses their insights into the child to develop their own professional understanding to enable the whole setting team to lead learning in this area:

> So, we're all sort of on the same page with what we're doing (about SLC). And our practice follows through right from baby room upwards. We use

and adapt the communication tools we've got from earlier and then follow through with the child.

Training about SLC is shared across the team. The manager and one of us went on a SLC course and then we had to come back and train the rest of the staff. It kind of it makes you feel more of a collective where if someone new came in, we all really share our ideas and knowledge, we bounce off each other. It's good that everyone's doing the same consistent thing with each child's communication. We wouldn't jump straight to a referral to the Speech and Language Therapist, we'd do a lot of work with the child first with their key person, we work through our own paperwork and try to find out as much information from the parents about their child's talking at home. It's something that builds up over years, but we're really lucky that we've got a really low staff turnover. We've all been here years as well. So, I think that really helps build bonds with parents and we've had siblings come and so we can get that bit more information about the child's communication needs that way as well.

REFLECTION 1.2

After reading Case Study 1.1 – practitioner insights, can you identify some key aspects of practice which support practitioner knowledge and skills within a setting?

Think about the strategies used and the key elements of practice in the setting which the practitioner identifies.

The section that follows will explore further aspects of leading practice to support children's speech and language development.

Developing the EY workforce – leadership within and beyond the setting

In the previous section, we noted the value of working together with parents. As members of a wider inter-agency team, it is also important to consider how we work with other actors in the child's C&L context. As discussed in the introduction and applied throughout this text, a theoretical framework which supports our thinking in this area is the ecological systems theory (EST) (Bronfenbrenner, 1977) (Figure 1.1).

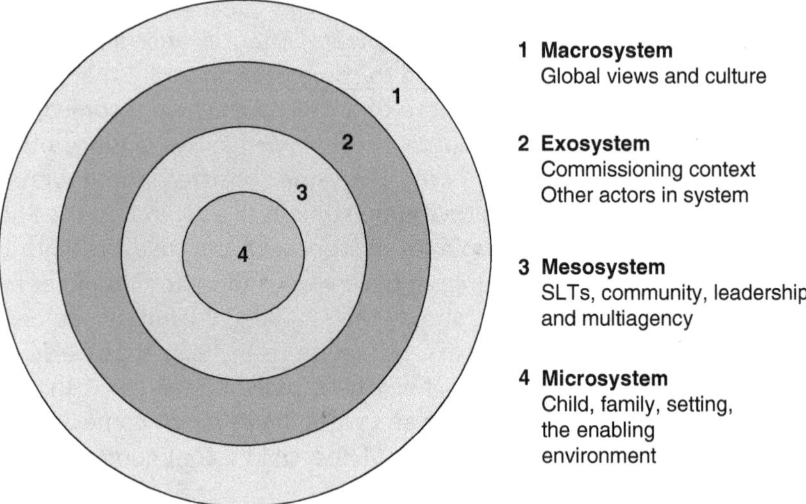

Figure 1.1 Bronfenbrenner ecological model (1979)

This theoretical framework considers the whole child, providing a sociocultural rather than psychological perspective on development. It proposes a two-way interaction between the child and their environment and includes the micro systems around the child as well as the interactions between families and professionals. From a wider systems view, the EST prompts consideration of the whole EY community and its wider macro policy and practice culture including the context and expectations for EYPs to be involved in inter-agency collaboration across health and education, for example.

REFLECTION 1.3

Consider a specific child in your setting.

- *Can you map out their own system?*
    - *Who is in it?*
    - *Who do you need to include or work with?*
    - *Whose knowledge will contribute to building a full picture of that child's C&L skills?*

Although as EYPs, it is helpful to think about systems in this way, research shows that sometimes the experience and skills of EYPs is not always heard within the system when services for children and families are being planned and developed

(Jovanovic et al., 2016). This research acknowledges the skills and knowledge of EYPs in relation to children's early communication but notes how their voices are often missing from the discussion about practice and policy to develop early support services for C&L, being driven instead by the judgements of policymakers and those who are not in daily practice. The case study which follows explores some aspects of this contradiction as experienced from the perspective of an EYP:

CASE STUDY 1.2 SUMMARY OF A DISCUSSION WITH AN EY PRACTITIONER AS PART OF A RESEARCH PROJECT

In talking to the practitioner about their knowledge and assessment of a child's SLCN, they explained their own level of confidence in providing assessment details to support the two-year assessment process. Explaining how the child had been at the setting since they were five months old, the practitioner detailed the robust tracking processes in the setting and the careful way in which evidence was built to support the concerns which they were expressing about the child's SLCN in the assessment report. The practitioner noted that, despite their expertise and knowledge of the child in question, it still felt difficult to have their voice recognised and that other actors in the system did not always value their assessment findings, judging them as less valid than those made by the health visitor, for example.

REFLECTION 1.4

Consider how to raise the profile of your own expertise; how can your team's voice be heard in shared assessments?

What connections can you make across a child's system to ensure meaningful inter-agency communication is supported?

With this in mind, there are a number of crucial aspects relating to leading good communication practice in the current context which support a systems approach to practice:

1 **Early identification** of C&L needs including participation in shared assessments such as the two-year progress check (DfE, 2022) and the Early Years Foundation Stage Profile (EYFSP) (DfE, 2023). EYPs are a key part of the early identification process. Their skills in working from positive child-led approaches in the Foundation Stage can support an assessment which focuses on the strengths and

needs rather than on diagnosis or labelling of a child. We need to purposefully take opportunities to contribute meaningfully to shared assessments and working together. For example, health visitors are key actors in the system and often the gatekeepers to services so developing ways to cooperate on the two-year check would be of great benefit to all involved.

2 **Communication-supporting environments** which move beyond focusing on verbal communication. While it is important to recognise the value of verbal communication in the development of a child's self-regulation and cognitive development (Vallotton and Ayoub, 2011), it is also of great value to think beyond spoken language. For example, Havighurst et al. (2019) support a consideration of the relationships which practitioners form with children which is worth reflecting on:

> *The social relationships educators forge with the young children in their care are foundational to learning and development, including early communication. A 'secure attachment relationship' is a term used to describe the bond between an educator who acts as the provider of safety, protection and understanding to individual children, and the child's responding feelings of being accepted, understood and supported by them. (p. 96)*

Research in Havighurst's paper explores a relational pedagogy, something which is also gaining prominence in the United Kingdom through the work of Grimmer (2021) where it is acknowledged that communication relationships are based on more than just modelling talk but also have a foundation on listening to children and understanding communication cues of all kinds, respect and respectful touch, care and spending time. Through not just our use of language but also through non-verbal means, we can develop reciprocity and communication in its widest sense.

REFLECTION 1.5

Consider these phrases taken directly from the Birth to 5 Matters non-statutory guidance (Early Education, 2021):

- *The key person helps the child to feel known, understood, cared about, and safe. (p. 30)*
- *Listening to children's voices and recognising these are expressed in a range of ways, including non-verbally, is central to inclusive practice. (p. 9)*

Consider the specific ways in which you and your team 'tune in' to children, communicating understanding and acceptance which can provide a spark to developing reciprocal interactions which may be verbal or non-verbal.

Challenge yourself to consider what you could do differently to improve your practice in this area.

3 **Parents** are central to shared working practices. Remember the aforementioned 2024 YouGov school readiness survey? Teachers' views on why children are not meeting milestones for SLC reflect their perspectives on parents and parenting and include parents not reading to children and parents spending time on electronic devices rather than talking with their children. In addition, teachers comment on the gap between the two-year check and starting school resulting in not enough in-depth developmental information for parents and a consequent lack of awareness in parental expectations around developmental milestones. Analysis of this survey provides a useful example of the way in which the wider systems around the child can influence their development, from the microsystem (Bronfenbrenner, 1977) in the home learning environment (HLE) to the broader community provision, guidance and relationships available between families and practitioners throughout children's earliest years. As part of the child's closest system, a trusted professional and a consistent link between home, education and the wider system, EYPs also need to be mindful of the temptation to blame parents for their child's SLCN. Montgomery and Cooper (2019) explore how parental expertise is being more valued and acknowledged in the current context but that there is still a clash about who knows best between parents and professionals. Parenting as a term has become laden with value judgements, and this is particularly evident in relation to C&L. As EYPs, access to parental knowledge is a strength which can be harnessed in the setting as we explore with families the things which they already know about their child's C&L.

4 **Continuing professional development (CPD) opportunities** as part of wider support systems. McDonald et al.'s 2015 study demonstrated that SLT training courses for EYPs had a positive effect on their use and application of communication strategies (PH England, 2020). Some of this training can be accessed, but there is also an opportunity for creativity in finding what's publicly available, often for free, that can be harnessed to support your own team development and CPD.

Resources to consider include:

- Tiny Happy People – a website all about early communication designed by SLTs for parents and useful for practitioners https://www.bbc.co.uk/tiny-happy-people.
- Professional websites which include access to free webinars, podcasts and useful practice articles.
- Your local NHS SLT website which may have practitioner and parent-facing resources to download and use.
- National charities such as Speech and Language UK, Makaton or The Sutton Trust which have downloadable resources on their websites.
- Research organisations such as the Education Endowment Foundation which provide free access to academic articles and evidence-based practice guidance and also offer opportunities for settings to sign up to participate in research studies.

REFLECTION 1.6

- *What resources could you use to develop CPD opportunities in your staff team?*
- *How could you set aside some teachable moments to incorporate these into ongoing CPD and sharing good practice in your team?*

CHAPTER SUMMARY

This chapter has highlighted the need for practitioners to consider communication in a wide sense beyond the individual child's spoken communication, encouraging a dedicated focus on all aspects of communication practice within and beyond the setting. As a leader, pedagogical leadership is modelling what works for children with the adults in the setting. If C&L is viewed in its widest sense, it is possible to develop an enabling communication environment for children, families and staff.

All staff need to recognise good practice with regard to C&L, practising skills they have learnt, engaging in peer support and knowing how to self-assess and assess the environment. In the context of the recognition of the importance of children's earliest learning experiences and the heightened expectations on educators in the Early Years to provide language-rich experiences, this chapter will have gone some way in supporting you to reflect on practice as well as to consider practical, structural and organisational elements which can be developed to harness and embed a consistent and flexible approach to communication in the setting.

KEY QUESTIONS

As we consider our leadership of communication practice in our settings, challenge yourself to reflect on the following and how you might develop spaces within your team to provide practical solutions:

- *Think about the language that children are exposed to in your setting – is it rich and descriptive?*
- *Do we alter the level of complexity as needed and allow time for the child to 'tune in'?*

- *How can you provide space to reflect on the quality and quantity of staff language?*
- *How do we support communication as a relationship?*
- *Are our communication relationships with our children authentic and holistic?*
- *Are we open to listen, learn and contain as well as to track, teach and talk?*
- *Are we tuning in to children as they communicate through all of the communicative methods they use?*
- *How could you develop systems to continually support and challenge communication practice within your setting?*
- *What do you want each adult and child to learn about communication as they come into contact with your provision?*

Further reading and resources

McQueen, D. and **Williams, J.** (2022). *Supporting the Development of Speech, Language and Communication in the Early Years*. UK: Jessica Kingsley.

This practice-focused test provides useful information including links and tools for developing good systems around practice and assessment and gives a speech and language therapist's perspective on working together in the Early Years.

https://pathway.thebalancedsystem.org/ [accessed 3/3/24]

This pathway is very useful in identifying wider aspect in the system where C&L support can be accessed for families and the staff team.

https://www.stokespeaks.org/ [accessed 3/3/24]

This community approach has been embedded in the local area in Stoke as an evidence-based example of good practice across the whole community.

https://tapestry.info/the-mandela-model-workbook-2.html [accessed 3/3/24]

This perspective is a useful model in supporting families to feel that they belong and their voices are heard in your setting.

2 TOTAL COMMUNICATION APPROACHES; USING SIGNS AND SYMBOLS

RACHAEL WEBSTER

THIS CHAPTER

By actively reading this chapter and engaging with the material, you will be able to:

- Identify a range of total communication strategies, approaches and interventions which can benefit children's communication and language development.
- Consider the use of specific total communication strategies, recognising when their implementation may or may not be suitable.
- Introduce some of the multiagency professionals who may be involved in the communication and language provision for children with Special Educational Needs and Disabilities (SEND) or Speech, Language and Communication Needs (SLCN) and the key principles surrounding effective working in partnership.
- Recognise the transient nature of popular strategies and the importance of effective evaluation of strategies prior to implementation.
- Begin to build your own 'Total communication toolkit' and consider how to utilise it to enhance your practice and delivery.

Introduction

The principles underpinning total communication environments are often thought to be established and universally understood, however as Morgan et al. (2019) observed, when we assume tacit knowledge, practitioners can be envisaging wildly different things. In specialist settings, staff may have experience and training in specific knowledge and interventions; however, these approaches are not always beneficial when universally applied, and the needs of the children will affect the features which make environments truly communication friendly.

With ever-increasing pressure on assessment results and a prevailing narrative of school-readiness (Hoskins and Smedley, 2019), Early Years practitioners would be forgiven for pursuing constant progression and implementing challenge in all areas, but actually the overarching message of this chapter is that

communication should be easy! Ensuring children have accessible means of communication helps equip them to engage in curriculum opportunities and demonstrate their understanding. A tendency for trends and short-lived initial excitement, combined with limited underpinning research, can create distrust or disinclination to implement specific strategies and, as ever within the early childhood sector access to training and commitment from leaders, as well as financial implications, will ultimately dictate the extent to which a setting is able or willing to adopt a strategy or approach. So here, the aim is to achieve a balance where we can identify and select symbolic communication strategies to create communication rich environments which respond to the needs of children and their communities. We must recognise that symbolic communication does not only relate to formal signing and symbol systems but also to the development of expressive and receptive language and use of informal images and gestures (Scott-Philips, 2015). Becoming more attuned to the prevalence of signs and symbols throughout our practice means, we can adapt our communication to make it inclusive for all children in the Early Years.

Symbolic language constructions and conventions

The way children develop language expression and comprehension is fundamental in our design of total communication approaches and environments. Even today, the nature/nurture debate continues to dominate much of the literature, although, as explored in chapter one, some more nuanced theoretical frameworks such as the sociolinguistic and psycholinguistic models have begun to have significant influence in pedagogical approaches to speech, language and communication (Johnson and White, 2020). These models recognise the complexity of language conventions and how quickly children begin to acquire them in their home language and the ease with which they adopt those of other languages. Certainly, some people believe humans have evolved to be hardwired for language development, as Chomsky (1976) proposed with his 'Language Acquisition Device' (LAD) theory. But not all languages have the same conventions and challenges, and English has been frequently identified as one of the most difficult to decipher due to sentence structure and word classification (Hanley, 2010; Hinkel, 2001). Ertem et al. (2018) found no significant variation in the pace of babies and young children's language development across four different countries which suggests that if we evolved a specific LAD, it is attuned to all languages.

subject – verb – object (SVO)	OR	subject – verb – information (SVI)
Bryony likes apple juice	OR	Billal ran fast

Table 2.1 Typical English sentence construction

Table 2.1 outlines the typical English sentence construction, however, with social interactions, we normally precede the subject with a greeting otherwise known as an interjection, e.g. *Hello Zainab!* This can be incredibly challenging, as we expect children to tune into the interaction without explicitly gaining their attention. As soon as children recognise and respond to their name at approximately six months, it becomes their indicator that information or instructions are forthcoming, particularly from familiar adults. But use of an interjection or a non-specific subject such as 'can you please tidy up?' does not give children enough warning to process and formulate a response, risking setting them up to fail. In our total communication environment, we should reconsider these established conventions and focus on the impact that even seemingly small interactions can have on children's perceptions of success in their everyday exchanges (Yoon and Templeton, 2019).

An overemphasis on manners has also been a long-standing feature of adult communications with young children, in Early Years settings and at home (Floyd et al., 2018). A common early interaction involves encouraging babies to say 'Ta' in response for an object, and they will very quickly begin to use this as a request when reaching for something. However, while many adults place a high value on manners, in real terms, the words *please* and *thank-you* hold no intrinsic meaning beyond social currency. Babies and young children use the word 'Ta' to indicate 'want' and receiving praise from adults for the perceived use of polite conventions. The most powerful expressive communication is the ability to say 'stop' and 'want' – this is also a vital element in our safeguarding duty to enable children to express dislike at the earliest opportunity (Franklin and Goff, 2019). This is not to say that manners are not important in communication development, but we should be mindful of the actual communication skills of the children in our care. For children with SLCN or those with SEND, focusing on manners is often not meaningful and can introduce additional complexities beyond their current functional communication levels. Our total communication practice should always be based on the children's needs rather than social sensibilities.

The communication environment

A total communication environment encompasses physical space, emotional connections and pedagogical approaches in addition to any specialist communication strategies for individual children with SEND (Beard, 2018). For some people, this is an environment rich in colour and imagery, saturated with celebrations of children and their cultures, but in 2009, Elizabeth Jarman published a framework for the creation of *Communication Friendly Spaces®* which is attributed for a trend towards more neutral colour pallets with limited decoration in an attempt to reduce over-stimulation and promote children's independent expression. However, this has led to a widely recreated template which some practitioners feel is dull and homogeneous with excessive use of beige and blond wood. Indeed, the trend has been criticised as solely an aesthetic choice (Caswell and Peach, 2022), with settings not always engaging in research to provide strong pedagogical basis for their design choices. It is difficult to claim the hessian backed boards in a baby's room enhance the children's learning environment when they are positioned above their eyeline.

When planning a total communication environment, start from the perspective of the children who will be using it. In fact, it helps to do this literally; have you ever looked around from ground level? Consider how they interact with the space and people within it, as well how they physically access it, being mindful of any physical impairments or sensory needs they may have. The need for distraction free environments for young children who experience sensory overload or have a visual impairment to be able to process information and formulate a response is well established (Wall, 2011), although most children need a balance. We can provide beautiful spaces where children feel valued and celebrated as members of the community and can see themselves represented through the display of their work or their photograph which help them grow into confident independent communicators with careful use of colour and contrast. Zoning calm areas and small spaces, both inside and outside, can enable children to take breaks and engage in focused tasks without limiting their communication potential.

Interprofessional working in total communication

It is important practitioners have a shared ethos to total communication within the setting and are working in partnership with agencies and families to ensure consistency of approaches. Children with SEND and SLCN may have several specialist professionals involved in planning and implementing communication strategies such as a Speech and Language Therapist (SLT), or a specialist SEND teaching service, who often works with families from the very earliest stages of identification. Practitioners should remember that our own experiences can help to plan appropriate communication strategies for children, but specialists will be able to accurately assess their needs and may have greater depth of knowledge of resources and interventions appropriate to their unique personal circumstances (Coupe-O'Kane and Goldbart, 2016).

CASE STUDY 2.1 ISAAC

Isaac is 3 years old. He was born with bilateral moderate congenital hearing impairment (HI) and wears a cochlear implant. He lives with his parents and two older sisters. He attends a local day nursery and is currently in the toddler room. His speech is delayed, and he has unclear pronunciation. The SLT has provided nursery with games and activities to help develop his speech sounds, recommending these are done several times daily with a small group of peers. It is challenging for nursery staff to incorporate the activities into daily routines and staff have expressed some scepticism towards the approach, feeling Issac is not making progress. His key person, Emilia, has spoken to Issac's dad, who wants to persevere with the SLT plan. Nursery staff do not see Isaac's mum who works away. They know that Issac's

(Continued)

(Continued)

hearing is an inherited condition, but his parents have never disclosed any difficulties relating to other family members. Emilia has previous experience working with children with HI and completed a British Sign Language (BSL) course, so she introduced Issac to signing in nursery and encouraging other staff to sign with him. He started to pick up vocabulary quickly and seems to find it easier, signing instead of talking at home and at nursery. Emilia believes this is beneficial as Isaac seems less frustrated when trying to make himself understood. The nursery manager received a letter from Isaac's dad requesting they stop using signing as it has created challenges at home; his mum has hearing and visual impairments so cannot see when he signs and Isaac is getting frustrated, hitting his mum when she does not immediately respond. The Manager is confused as she was unaware staff had been signing with him and feels the time spent on introducing BSL could have been used to implement the SLT activities instead.

REFLECTION 2.1

- *What are the potential long-term impacts of this inconsistency of approach for Isaac and his family?*
- *How could professionals have worked more effectively together from the beginning of Isaac's time at nursery?*
- *How could Emilia's knowledge have been harnessed and implemented in a more strategic way for Issac and his family?*

Signing

Makaton and Sign-along are established common forms of signing, both based on BSL. They are examples of 'Sign Supported English' (SSE) which is widely used to help children and adults with SLCN/SEND to understand and express keywords. It provides concrete visual cues to help decipher spoken language, which is momentary and invisible (Winsler et al., 2018). The fundamental factor in successful implementation of signs and symbols surrounds the level of symbolic understanding which the children have and their developmental trajectory. It is tempting to consider signs and symbols a universal panacea where children exhibit some degree of communication need or delay, including, EAL but the overuse of these strategies can prove ineffective and, in some cases, actually detrimental, particularly for children with visual impairments or multiple disabilities.

Both signing and symbols (or photographs) create additional visual information which learners need to process, interpret and respond to in order to formulate an appropriate response. For children who are not yet communicating at symbolic levels this additional information can become distracting and create visual noise (Morris, 2018).

Accurate assessment is vital therefore when planning a communication environment. The Early Years Foundation Stage (EYFS) (DfE, 2024) and Development Matters (DfE, 2023a) both provide communication assessment milestones, but these are holistic models which assume a typical development trajectory and sequence for most children where symbolic communication begins naturally at around the same time they start to respond to their own reflection. It can be difficult for practitioners and parents to understand symbolic progression in isolation, but published tools such as the Communication Matrix and the Early Communication Assessment can be very useful in accurately discerning children's symbolic awareness and deciding when to introduce signs and symbols to develop a framework for symbolic progression. Information on both these tools can be found in the further reading and resources section of this chapter.

Baby-signing grew from SSE, under the premise that infants understand more than they can express and may exhibit frustration as their spoken communication development catches up with their comprehension. Adopters of this strategy believe teaching signing right from a baby's first few months will enable them to effectively communicate likes, wants and emotions significantly before they develop equivalent abilities via spoken word, accelerating their speech language and communication (Kusters and Lucas, 2022). There is evidence supporting this, although it is limited and does not show significant impact for long-term language development. Importantly though, the converse concern that it may impair speech development has been dispelled (Lederer, 2018). Practitioners have reported early introduction to signing for babies supports awareness of varying communication needs of their peers and may promote more inclusive communication from the outset. For parents and carers, this rationale may be less compelling as it is not necessarily directly associated with outcomes for their child, but baby-signing can also support emotional communication through the enhanced responsiveness of parents and carers (Freeman, 2022).

Symbols in the environment

Use of symbols, particularly those associated with Makaton or Widget symbol writing software, has become commonplace in early years settings, emulating established practices in special schools. Labels displaying photos and symbols of the contents of every box or cupboard can be beneficial for children to access resources independently and in particular help children for whom these strategies have been recommended by specialist SEND services or SLT. There are potential difficulties in adopting symbols as a universal approach, particularly when there are children using the setting who are not yet communicating a symbolic level. It is vital to consider the definition of 'symbols' and recognise the full range of experiences which it encompasses; symbols are something intended to represent a concept, object or experience and communicate a shared understanding. So, we also need to consider photographs and illustrations as well as text and spoken words.

For learners with profound or complex communication needs whose symbolic communication is at an earlier stage, it may not be possible to ascribe meaning to third-party abstract symbols such as a word or image (Bond and Navarro, 2023). Environmental cues can be powerful examples of early symbolic communication that we continue to use throughout our lives regardless of our communication need or abilities (Coupe and O'Kane, 2016). The sound of the kettle boiling might mean a cup of coffee is forthcoming, but the same message could be conveyed by the smell as it brews. Most people have the complex ability to decode a number of symbols which could indicate a similar meaning: the word 'coffee', the sight of the jar, the logo for a high street coffee shop or even a specific time of day, can hold shared symbolic understanding of the concept 'coffee'. For someone communicating at pre-intentional levels, however, this transference of meaning is not internalised during the course of our language development. It is the communication partners who need to identify particular cues which hold meaning for individual children and keep repeating them alongside the experience until meaning is retained. Over time, the child might start showing recognition or even anticipation when they encounter the cue, which would indicate early awareness of shared understanding.

Symbolism of songs, rhymes and stories

Gestural communication can enhance children's ability to learn, retain and recall information. Of course, this includes signing systems but also relates to less formal gestures that we associate commonly with action songs and rhymes and the physical retelling of familiar stories. We twiddle our fingers as Incy Wincy Spider climbs the waterspout or pull and clap as we wind the bobbin up, understanding that these songs and rhymes with strong repetition and clearly measured rhythm are beneficial to language development and phonological awareness of children. But babies can often participate in the associated actions with a high degree of fluency several months before they can repeat the lyrics, and for children new to English (NTE), these activities can be emulated often before any secure vocabulary is uttered (Davidson, 2015). Gestures and actions help create a shared language, without the complexities of spoken words, utilising visual understanding by providing a model to copy. The fact that in stories and rhymes actions are often repeated several times, and we frequently revisit stories and rhymes which children appear to find most engaging, enables them to become familiar with the actions, rehearse them in a group without individual pressure and receive affirmation for their engagement. Once they retain actions, often words will come more easily with a clear framework on which to construct them. SSE has the potential for similar success; however, it can lack frequent repetition and the informal enjoyable activity in which learning takes place. Many BSL signs are, by necessity abstract without obvious connection to the subject making them harder to retain and repeat or practice. It is the signs that hold meaning for the individual child, or which are embedded into clear routines which children learn, retain, and use spontaneously in the setting or at home.

CASE STUDY 2.2 AVALIE

Avalie is three. She came to England as a refugee from Iran with her mother, father and four older siblings 10 weeks ago. She has never lived in an English-speaking country and her family are NTE. They live in a hostel with other refugee families, and Avalie has not been able to enrol in nursery yet. Very few other families speak Persian, and there are no safe spaces for Avalie and her siblings to play with other children. Carla and David from the Early Years Outreach team come to visit the hostel twice a week. They bring a selection of children's books with puppets and finish each session with a story. The books are all in English because they do not have dual language books for all languages spoken. Today, it is Avelie's turn to choose the story; she looks through the books and finds 'We're going on a Bear Hunt' with the bear puppet. Passing it to Carla, Avalie makes claw shapes with her hands and growls loudly like a bear, smiling. Throughout the story, Avalie joins in with actions and makes sounds with many of the other children. At the end of the session, while Carla and David are tidying, Avalie picks up the book and the bear and pretends to read the story to the group. She chatters away in Persian, turning the pages and doing the actions with the sounds for each part of the story. Some children gather around Avalie and join in with the actions and sounds. At the end, they pretend to run away and fall on the ground laughing. David gives Avalie a big round of applause and laughs happily.

REFLECTION 2.2

- *Why do you think Avalie was able to choose a favourite book from the selection even though they were all English texts?*
- *Consider the symbols within a familiar story; why were all the children able to join in and share the specific experiences despite speaking different home languages?*
- *How do you think Avalie might feel when other children join in with her story, or when David gives her a round of applause?*
- *Can you think some other examples where repeated actions, sounds and phrases could be embedded into routines to support shared understanding?*

Engaging in storytelling is an intrinsic aspect of human communication (Landrum et al., 2019), and children with SLCN can experience significant barriers accessing narrative, songs and rhymes which can have a compounding effect on their communication development; in addition to their SLCN, they are also unable to engage independently in experiences which proved so beneficial to Avalie and her peers. However, highly adaptive approaches enable all children, including those with the most severe learning disabilities, to participate in stories and songs in meaningful ways (Doak, 2023). Puppets and soft toys are commonly used in interactive story telling experiences, but for children with visual impairments and learning disabilities, these representations do not actually allow for multi-sensory engagement as they tend to all feel similar and do not provide any distinct features associated with the individual aspects of the story. A soft toy will always feel like a soft toy. But the use of sensory stories can prove incredibly powerful for children with visual impairments or complex learning needs. A typical sensory story includes a reduced version of a published text paired with stimuli for each aspect presented in sequence for children to explore. Preece and Zhao (2015) found them beneficial in developing memory skills and focused attention and promoting anticipation. It is important to consider the individual features of the story and choose elements which provide meaningful, distinct sensory experiences (Grace and Longhorn, 2015). Where possible, real resources are best such as stones, water or bark. But when considering animals or imaginary monsters, we have to select resources which capture something specific – a whale is big, smooth, and always wet; a gym mat sprayed with water could prove a much more relevant and interesting experience than a toy whale.

Assistive technology can enhance engagement in narrative experiences. We can purchase talking picture books with audible cues recorded on integrated buttons or panels, but we can also create our own relatively cheaply using widely available resources from education distribution companies such as *Talking Point buttons* and *Talking Panels.* This can also enable children to develop their symbolic expression through creating and articulating their own stories; even for children with profound and complex learning needs, Doak (2023) found they could engage in a degree of co-authorship through showing preferences and making choices using story making apps on mobile technologies.

CHAPTER SUMMARY

Symbolic communication is a complex aspect of child development, where there is still much which is unknown or contested. However, by recognising the breadth of symbolic communication in all its forms and how children use both formal and informal symbols to understand and express themselves, practitioners can create inclusive and empowering communication environments. By making some subtle changes to the way we use expressive language with children and questioning established communication conventions such as the way we address children and our expectations of their responses, as well as how we can design our spaces, we can truly promote children's understanding and expression.

Practitioners should recognise that their knowledge of children's SLCN need to be developed in partnership with a range of professionals and families, and it is important that we aim to continuously progress our knowledge and expertise as it is often when we believe we know the answers that practice begins to suffer and we can lose the intentions behind our actions as some people believe happened with beige décor in recent years. Most importantly, we should be aware that the pedagogies which underpin how we design our Early Years spaces and interventions should be morphing to the ever-changing needs of our children. The typical conceptualisation of signs and symbols as being based on SSE and Widget symbols needs to be reframed to understand symbolic communication in its broader context, where these are elements of a broader toolkit which need to be planned at a micro level and cannot always be applied universally.

KEY QUESTIONS

When we begin to review our total communication practice and our use of signing and symbols with young children, it is important to reflect on how this could be implemented throughout the physical and emotional environment in our settings; consider these questions and examine how you and your colleagues could work together to practically support children's communication development:

- *How will you assess children's symbolic communication skills and ensure the most appropriate strategies are provided either individually or throughout the environment?*
- *Can you recognise any aspects of your own interactions with young children which may be confusing or detrimental to their ability to process information and formulate an appropriate response?*
- *How can you ensure you are using strong pedagogical principles and apply them appropriately when planning your physical environment to facilitate the communication needs of the individual children who will be using it?*
- *How effective is our partnership with parents, families and other professional in planning and implementing appropriate individual communication devices and strategies, and how could it be developed?*

Further reading and resources

Education Endowment Foundation: Early Years Toolkit: https://educationendowmentfoundation.org.uk/education-evidence/early-years-toolkit/communication-and-language-approaches

Resources and tools to support communication and language approaches.

Department for Education: Help for early years providers: https://help-for-early-years-providers.education.gov.uk/communication-and-language/interactions

Resources for Early Years providers around communication and language.

The Sensory Projects https://www.thesensoryprojects.co.uk/

Resources and tools to support inclusive communication education.

NASEN Whole School SEND: Communication and Interaction https://www.wholeschoolsend.org.uk/page/communication-and-interaction

High quality information, resources and CPD to support a whole school approach to inclusion.

www.communicationmatrix.org [accessed on 13/5/22]

A nonprofit project devoted to improving outcomes for individuals with complex communication needs around the world.

Coupe-O'Kane, J. and **Goldbart, J. (2016).** *Communication before Speech: Development and Assessment*. 2nd ed. London: Routledge.

Coupe-O'Kane and Goldbart address the theoretical aspects of the development of communication and detail their assessment method.

3 NAVIGATING THE DIGITAL LANDSCAPE: SUPPORTING YOUNG CHILDREN'S SPEECH AND LANGUAGE DEVELOPMENT IN EARLY YEARS SETTINGS

MICHELLE BUGBY

THIS CHAPTER

By actively reading this chapter and engaging with the material, you will be able to:

- Understand how various digital tools and platforms can influence young children's speech and language acquisition.
- Examine what digital technologies offer children in terms of developmental support and linguistic growth.
- Investigate specific elements within digital applications and devices that promote language development and vocabulary expansion.
- Consider how to effectively incorporate digital technologies into educational settings to support speech and language development.
- Reflect on how and when early childhood practitioners should interact with children to maximise the benefits of technology in learning environments.
- Explore the potential challenges, ethical issues and considerations related to screen time, privacy and equitable access to digital resources for all children.

Introduction

In this chapter, we undertake an analytical exploration of the potential advantages, challenges and practical dimensions surrounding the incorporation of technology into the realm of speech and language development among young children. The influences for and against the use of technology in young children's education appears to be concerned with the quality of the experiences. A key question to be explored is what value technology brings and what speech and language affordances they offer to those children in the formative early years?

The role of technology in early childhood education?

In today's digitally driven world, technology has seamlessly woven itself into the fabric of early childhood education (Palaiologou, 2016; Vidal-Hall et al., 2020). During their critical stages of language acquisition and communication development, young children encounter a diverse array of learning opportunities through digital platforms. The gradual introduction of technologies like iPads and tablets into Early Years settings signifies a compelling albeit gradual evolution, offering innovative avenues for early language development and experiences (Arnott et al., 2019).

Research has consistently demonstrated the potential benefits of digital technologies in early childhood settings (Fleer, 2018; Furenes et al., 2021), with early childhood practitioners finding the versatility of tablets and digital technology highly appealing, as they seek innovative methods to revitalise their teaching approaches (Billington, 2016).

Murcia et al. (2018) assert that the integration of digital technology enhances social inclusivity and learning outcomes in both formal and informal environments, while also enabling personalised support. Despite this, concerns regarding the suitability of these technologies for young children persist (Dubicka et al., 2019), with one in four early childhood educators in the United Kingdom believing that there is no place for digital technology in early childhood settings (Billington, 2016). The key concerns are the potential for over-reliance on technology and the need for children to develop other skills, such as speech and language, social interaction and forming positive relationships (Crowe et al., 2017). Aligning with this thought process, Arnott (2016, p.87) contends that while digital play holds significance, it should not overshadow other vital components within the educational framework.

One questions if children do not have the opportunities to acquire the fundamental skills in navigating through a digital landscape, will they find themselves unable to participate and communicate in the social, economic and cultural life around them (OECD, 2015, p.15)? For children to be able to participate in a modern society, it is essential for early childhood educators to identify and promote interventions related to early academic success (Bostock, 2020).

REFLECTION 3.1

- *How do you perceive the role of technology in early childhood development?*
- *In what ways do you observe technology influencing children's language, play and exploration?*

Evaluating the role of technology

For children living in a contemporary culture, ways of being and acting in the social world are framed by their experiences with new digital technologies. This exposure creates different dispositions and orientations to learning and thinking, by empowering and constructing new concepts of work and play (Clark and Picton, 2019). While technology offers valuable opportunities for learning and engagement, it must be integrated carefully alongside traditional pedagogical practices to ensure a balanced and holistic approach to early childhood education. The engagement in using digital technologies occurs at a critical period in children's lives where they start to learn a wide range of skills and develop their identities as effective and competent learners.

Technology serves as a valuable resource in providing diverse linguistic experiences, facilitating both the acquisition of a first language and the introduction of new languages to children, particularly those from different language backgrounds (van der Westhuizen and Hannaway, 2021). While there is evidence that children enjoy using technology, such as touch screen mobile devices and of their correlation on positive outcomes on children's speech and language develop, learning and educational engagement (Barzillai et al., 2018), it is important to recognise that the use of technology does not automatically lead to meaningful learning. Merely possessing technological proficiency does not guarantee a child's comprehension of literacy content.

Consequently, it is crucial to exercise critical thought to ensure that technology is developmentally appropriate for young children and can be seamlessly integrated into their learning experiences (Billington, 2016). Early childhood educators must prioritise children's developmental stages when integrating technology into early learning environments. This entails evaluating what fosters healthy child development before determining how technology can enhance learning outcomes. Reflecting on these considerations, you could think about the following questions to enhance your integration of technology in your teaching practices:

REFLECTION 3.2

- *In what ways can you leverage technology to provide diverse linguistic experiences that support the acquisition of both first and additional languages, particularly for children from different language backgrounds?*
- *What criteria and considerations could you use to evaluate the developmental appropriateness of technology in your early learning environments, ensuring it enhances rather than hinders healthy child development and learning outcomes?*

Thoughtful integration of technology

Thoughtful integration of technology tailored to children's developmental stages can significantly contribute to their growth and learning, particularly when families and early years educators take an active role (Johnston et al., 2018). For learning to be really effective, practitioners should recognise the considerable amount of learning that occurs outside the setting, as learning happens all of the time and is influenced by the environment, culture, people and situations. It is important for early childhood educators to acknowledge children's prior knowledge and home experiences of digital technologies before they can begin to support and plan for children's speech and language development and to work with parents so they understand how the technology is used with the children at the setting (Johnston et al., 2018). Adopting a 'one-size-fits-all' approach is ineffective when integrating technology into early childhood learning environments. Prioritising children's developmental stages and assessing the suitability of technology necessitates evaluating factors that foster healthy child development, before determining how technology can enhance learning outcomes.

The three Cs: content, context and child-centredness

To guide this assessment, consideration of the three Cs, content, context and child-centredness, can be instrumental (Guernsey, 2012).

- Content: How does this technology facilitate young children's learning, engagement, expression, imagination or exploration?
- Context: What social interactions, such as conversations with early childhood educators or peers, occur before, during and after the use of the technology? Does it complement children's language, learning experiences and natural play patterns without causing interruptions?
- Child-Centred: What does this particular child require at this moment to support their speech and language growth and development? Is this technology aligned with the child's needs, abilities, interests and developmental stage?

Enhancing learning through technology

The integration of technology into speech and language developmental programmes offers numerous advantages, including enhanced accessibility to customised learning experiences, allowing educational content to be tailored to the individual needs and preferences of young learners, thereby facilitating personalised learning pathways. The versatility of tablets and mobile digital devices has enabled an 'anywhere, anytime' approach to learning (Billington, 2016). This flexibility accommodates children's individual interests, offering opportunities for personalised and enriched language and communication experiences, fostering the idea that users can practice and enhance their language skills at their convenience and across diverse settings. Therefore, applications (apps) are designed to be flexible and adaptable, allowing for customisation based on each child's unique learning profile. Selecting high-quality and developmentally appropriate technology-based resources is crucial for supporting children's language development because when they are aligned with learning intentions, they can effectively support children's language development by targeting key skills and concepts.

Additionally, interactive digital platforms create dynamic and immersive learning environments, encouraging active participation and fostering motivation (Vidal-Hall et al., 2020). Through gamified activities and multimedia resources, technology captures children's interest and sustains their engagement in speech and language exercises. Interactive learning applications, in particular, have revolutionised speech and language engagement by offering diverse modes of learning, including visual, auditory and kinaesthetic elements. Crafted with meticulous attention to user experience, these applications facilitate real-time and active participation through intuitive features such as swiping, tapping and providing immediate feedback on pronunciation and grammar (Furenes et al., 2021; Tan et al., 2013). Children tend to remember information better when engaged in digital play that involves auditory and visual stimuli. By participating in interactive digital activities that encourage verbal expression, children have the opportunity to strengthen their ability to communicate effectively. Digital play aids in the development of communication skills as it encourages children to formulate questions, improve vocabulary and listen attentively during play activities (van der Westhuizen and Hannaway, 2021). These features actively engage children in language activities, making the learning process both enjoyable and theoretically more effective. This form of play not only enhances memory but also contributes to the development of communication skills, providing opportunities to increase their vocabulary, sentence structure and their general understanding of semantics (Snow and Matthews, 2016). Undoubtedly, technology revolutionises the ways in which children play and can significantly enhance their learning experiences.

Children become literate in many ways, not just through language but through learning to use a combination of different modes, such as gaze, gesture, image, movement, layout, music and sound effects (Cremin et al., 2022). For example, language applications often include interactive games and stories where children can interact with on-screen objects to hear vocabulary pronounced, reinforcing their language acquisition (Furenes et al., 2021). Technologies allow children to keep up with the fast-paced digital world and help them gain visual-reasoning skills. For example, My Story is a creative literacy application that enables children to produce their own stories. The application has easy-to-follow icons and therefore is simple to use. Alongside the text, the children can insert photographs, create their own drawings, or use image clips that are embedded in the app (Marsh et al., 2015). It encompasses all the skills, knowledge and dispositions that children develop towards printed, visual, spoken and digital texts. Features such as question prompts and animated elements in digital technologies can also support vocabulary growth (Liu et al., 2024). Neumann's (2014, p. 7) findings suggested the 'tactile nature of the tablet allows young children to engage in activities such as tracing letter shapes with a finger while listening to letter sounds, which may foster their learning'. Highlighting this multi-sensory engagement has the potential to enhance children's learning experiences and promotes their speech and language development.

Adaptive technologies and personalised learning platforms exemplify this approach by dynamically adjusting the level of difficulty and pacing of activities in response to individual children's progress (van der Westhuizen and Hannaway, 2021). For example, a language learning application might adapt its content based on a child's performance, gradually increasing complexity as the child demonstrates proficiency or providing additional support when encountering difficulties. This adaptive nature ensures that children are appropriately challenged while receiving targeted support and scaffolding as needed. This interdisciplinary approach enhances children's overall speech and language abilities. To reflect on the integration of technology in enhancing learning, you could consider the following questions:

REFLECTION 3.3

- *How can we ensure that the digital technologies we use are aligned with the individual learning needs and developmental stages of the children in our care?*
- *In what ways can we balance the use of interactive digital platforms with traditional teaching methods to foster a holistic learning environment?*
- *How can we measure and evaluate the effectiveness of adaptive technologies in supporting children's speech and language development?*

Challenges of technology integration

Despite its potential benefits, the integration of technology into speech and language development initiatives is not without challenges. One of the foremost concerns is the risk of overreliance on technology, which may diminish opportunities for authentic face-to-face communication and interpersonal interaction (van der Westhuizen and Hannaway, 2021). Excessive screen time and passive consumption of digital content can impede language acquisition and hinder the development of critical communication skills, such as turn-taking and social reciprocity. Additionally, Crowe et al. (2017) identified the repetition of the same application or game could be seen as a barrier over time because it could lead to a decrease in children's engagement and motivation to participate. Children may also experience a sense of frustration and low self-esteem after several failures in playing digital interactive games, which could negatively impact their feelings, the overall quality of the game and its success.

Human interaction remains paramount for children to adapt and learn language effectively; consequently, technology should not replace human interaction but rather serve as a facilitator to enhance speech and language development by providing additional avenues for language exploration and practice. Bostock (2020) reinforces this notion, suggesting that children perceive technology as an enhancement rather than a replacement for teacher interaction. Children value the personal touch and responsive communication provided by early childhood educators, while also recognising the benefits of technology in reinforcing learning, accessing resources and receiving immediate feedback (Clark and Picton, 2019). Early childhood educators serve as vital guides in assisting children to assign meaning to what they hear, see and experience while using technology, thereby significantly contributing to language comprehension and development (Eng et al., 2020). Through thoughtful facilitation and scaffolding, early childhood educators can help children navigate digital platforms, interpret audiovisual content and make connections between their experiences in the virtual world and their real-life interactions. By fostering dialogue, asking open-ended questions and providing contextually relevant explanations, early childhood educators create opportunities for children to construct meaning, expand their vocabulary and refine their language skills in both digital and real-life contexts. For example, early years educators can design cross-curricular projects that involve using digital tools to create multimedia presentations, write digital stories or conduct virtual research, thereby enhancing language skills while also developing digital literacy, creativity and critical thinking abilities. This collaborative approach not only enhances children's linguistic competence but prepares them to effectively navigate the complexities of today's digitally driven world (Clark and Picton, 2019).

A reality is that a significant portion of children are deeply immersed in a digital world, where digital games hold substantial potential to enrich language teaching. However, it is crucial to acknowledge that not all children in the United Kingdom have equal access to digital devices and data. The digital divide remains wide (Holmes and Burgess, 2022), posing limitations on access for many children. Equitable access to technology is essential in ensuring that all children, regardless of socio-economic background or educational needs, have equal opportunities to benefit from technology-based speech and language interventions (van der Westhuizen and Hannaway, 2021). Early childhood educators can address the digital divide by advocating for increased funding and resources to provide digital devices and internet access to underserved communities. Additionally, they can integrate technology into their curriculum in inclusive ways, ensuring that digital learning experiences are accessible and beneficial for all children, regardless of their socio-economic background or educational needs.

The proliferation of educational applications and digital games poses significant challenges for early childhood educators, who must discern between effective, evidence-based interventions and entertainment driven content. Navigating this vast landscape requires early educators to identify materials that not only align with educational objectives but also meet individual developmental needs of children. Furthermore, the absence of clear curriculum recommendations regarding the integration of digital learning programmes and games in language teaching complicates educators' efforts to leverage technology effectively for language development. To address these challenges, targeted professional development and curriculum enhancements are essential, enabling early childhood educators to unlock the full potential of digital tools in supporting language acquisition and development.

REFLECTION 3.4

- *How do we evaluate the quality and appropriateness of the digital based resources we use?*
- *Are the apps and digital tools aligned with evidence-based practices and tailored to children's individual learning needs?*
- *How can we ensure that the content we use effectively supports children's language development and learning outcomes?*

Flexibility and personalisation

Technology serves as a powerful tool for augmentative and alternative communication (AAC) for children with speech and language impairments. Speech-generating devices and communication apps empower non-verbal or minimally verbal children to express themselves effectively, thereby promoting social interaction and linguistic development (Iacono et al., 2016). AAC encompasses various strategies and tools designed to supplement or replace traditional spoken communication for children with challenges in speech production or comprehension (Elsahar et al., 2019). Among these tools, speech-generating devices (SGDs) and communication applications stand out as pivotal advancements.

SGDs, often referred to as electronic communication aids, are specialised devices capable of generating audible or visual messages based on user input. These devices range from simple button-based systems to sophisticated touchscreen interfaces, offering users a spectrum of options tailored to their abilities and needs (Soomro and Soomro, 2018). By providing a means to express thoughts, needs and emotions, SGDs empower nonverbal or minimally verbal children to communicate effectively, fostering independence and enhancing their quality of life. To illustrate the profound impact of such technology, consider the following case study:

CASE STUDY 3.1 EMILY

Emily is a four-year-old girl with severe apraxia of speech, a condition that significantly impairs her ability to produce spoken language. She has strong cognitive abilities but has found communicating her wants, needs and thoughts verbally difficult, leading to frustration and social isolation in her Early Years setting.

To support Emily's communication development, her educators introduced her to a tablet equipped with a communication application (app) tailored to her needs. The app featured a personalised grid layout with picture symbols representing common words, phrases and concepts. With guidance from her speech and language therapist (SLT), Emily learnt to navigate the app, selecting symbols to form sentences and express herself.

Through consistent use of the communication app, Emily gradually improved her ability to express herself effectively, bridging the gap between her thoughts and verbal expression. The personalised nature of the app allowed Emily to engage with relevant vocabulary and concepts tailored to her needs and interests, further enhancing her communication skills. Over time, Emily's confidence in using the app grew, enabling her to initiate conversations, make choices independently and advocate for herself more assertively. Additionally, the social interactions facilitated by the tablet helped Emily forge meaningful connections with her peers and educators, promoting her social–emotional development alongside her linguistic progress. As a result, Emily's overall speech, language and communication abilities flourished, empowering her to participate more fully in activities and interact with confidence in her Early Years setting.

Emily's story provides an example how technology enhances communication skills and offers diverse linguistic experiences through interactive digital play. Adaptive technologies provide personalised learning, ensuring appropriate challenge and support. Early childhood educators should therefore prioritise children's developmental stages, ensuring tailored and thoughtful integration of technology, informed by evidence-based practices. To further explore the implications of technology integration, consider the following reflective questions:

REFLECTION 3.5

- *How equitable is access to technology in your Early Years setting?*
- *What barriers or inequalities in access need to be addressed to ensure all children have equal opportunities?*
- *How can we promote equitable access to technology for children from diverse backgrounds and with varying needs?*

Importance of professional development

The early childhood education sector faces a pressing need for comprehensive guidance, support and training at both local and national levels to maximise the potential of technology in enhancing teaching practices. While technology is often integrated into current teaching methods, its full potential remains underutilised due to the lack of structured support for educators. There is a clear imperative for purposeful training and informative guidance tailored to the unique needs of early childhood educators, empowering them to creatively harness the benefits of technology in their classrooms. By providing educators with the necessary tools, resources and professional development opportunities, policymakers and educational leaders can foster a culture of innovation and excellence in Early Years settings, ensuring that technology is effectively leveraged to support children's holistic development. Early childhood educators may be apprehensive about their own digital literacy skills and their ability to effectively integrate technology into existing curriculum frameworks. Providing professional development opportunities is crucial for enhancing practitioners' digital literacy skills and pedagogical knowledge related to technology integration. Early Years settings should offer training and support to empower practitioners to effectively integrate technology into their teaching practices and address any challenges or concerns that arise. To illustrate the transformative impact of professional development, consider the following case study:

CASE STUDY 3.2 SARAH

Sarah, an early childhood educator, initially hesitated to integrate technology into her teaching due to concerns about screen time and uncertainty about its effectiveness. To address her reservations, she attended professional development training focused on technology in early childhood education.

During the training, Sarah learnt practical strategies for incorporating age-appropriate digital resources into her teaching, aimed at scaffolding young children's speech and language development. She gained confidence and returned to her setting eager to implement what she had learnt, introducing educational apps and interactive games aligned with speech and language learning objectives.

Over time, Sarah observed positive impacts on the children's speech and language development. Technology engaged reluctant learners and complemented traditional teaching methods, providing opportunities for personalised learning experiences and effective progress tracking.

Through her journey of professional development, Sarah transformed into a champion of technology integration in Early Years education, emphasising responsible use and innovative approaches to support speech and language development effectively.

This case study highlights the significance of professional development for Early Years educators to effectively integrating technology into teaching practices. Through targeted training, Sarah gained the knowledge, skills and confidence needed to integrate technology for speech and language development in her classroom. Professional development facilitated Sarah's transition from scepticism to enthusiasm, demonstrating how ongoing learning opportunities empower educators to adapt to changing educational landscapes, enhance teaching strategies and ultimately improve learning outcomes for children. To further reflect on the importance of professional development and its impact on technology integration, consider the following reflective questions:

REFLECTION 3.6

- *What professional development opportunities are available to enhance your digital literacy skills and pedagogical knowledge?*
- *What strategies can you implement to address challenges or concerns related to technology integration?*
- *How do you address concerns about children's privacy, screen time and exposure to potentially harmful content?*

CHAPTER SUMMARY

This chapter delved into the intricate relationship between technology and speech and language development in early childhood education. In today's digitally driven world, technology has become an integral part of early childhood education, offering innovative avenues for speech and language development. However, despite its potential benefits, concerns about overreliance on technology and its suitability for young children persist. While technology offers valuable opportunities for learning and engagement, it must be integrated carefully alongside traditional pedagogical practices to ensure a balanced and holistic approach. Professional development plays a crucial role in empowering educators to navigate these complexities and effectively integrate technology into their teaching practices. The lack of guidance, support and training from local and national levels needs to be addressed, as technology is often assimilated to current teaching practices, yet greater use can be made of its potential if early childhood educators are supported in its creative use, highlighting the essential need in the Early Years sector for purposeful training and informative guidance. Through targeted training

(Continued)

(Continued)

and ongoing support, educators can harness the full potential of technology to support speech and language development, fostering children's communication skills and preparing them for success in a digital world. For children's learning experiences to be rewarding, early childhood practitioners need to provide sensitive support and carefully weave digital technology innovatively into the fabric of their practice and within the broader context of children's learning. As Flewitt et al. (2015, p.17) point out, if innovative uses of technologies continue to remain absent from young children's learning, 'then we risk failing to turn on a powerful switch that can light up this generation's learning'.

KEY QUESTIONS

After engaging with the content of this chapter, consider the following:

- *What are your views on the use of technology with young children?*
- *Do you feel that young children are disadvantaged through the prevalence of technology?*
- *What would you say to parents who asked your advice on whether they should purchase a device for their three-year-old?*

Further reading and resources

Stephen, C. Brooker, L. Oberhuemer, P. and **Parker-Rees, R.** (2019). *Digital Play and Technologies in the Early Years* (eds). Abingdon, Oxon: Routledge.

Kaye, L. (2016). *Young Children in a Digital Age: Supporting Learning and Development with Technology in Early Years*. Abingdon, Oxon: Routledge.

Learning applications

As highlighted by the Department for Education (2020), recommendations such as the six applications available on the Hungry Little Minds website offer tailored solutions for different age groups and learning needs.

Lingumi (For children aged 2-5): Sets of learning games, speech recognition games and video-based games to help with a child's grammar and getting them speaking their first words early on.

Kaligo (For children aged 3-5): The first digital handwriting exercise book using a stylus and tablet, built using AI and co-created with teachers, occupational therapists and neuroscientists.

Phonics Hero (For school-aged children): Over 850 fun, varied and motivating games take a child step by step through the 44 sounds, the reading and spelling of words and how to conquer sentences.

Teach Your Monster to Read (For school-aged children): Covers the first two years of learning to read, from matching letters and sounds to enjoying little books, designed in collaboration with leading academics.

Navigo Game (For school-aged children): Focuses on developing skills that underpin reading, including phonics, letters and sounds, designed by UCL Institute of Education and Fish in a Bottle.

Fonetti (For school-aged children): The world's first 'Listening Bookshop' interacting with children by giving visual cues in real time as they read aloud and highlighting where the most support is needed.

4 THE IMPACTS OF OUTDOOR PEDAGOGY ON CHILDREN'S COMMUNICATION

TANYA RICHARDSON

THIS CHAPTER

By actively reading this chapter and engaging with the material, you will be able to:

- Explore the impact of nature and the outdoors on communication and language development.
- Consider what different environments can offer children developmentally.
- Explore what elements within an outdoor environment prompt language learning and vocabulary.
- Consider practical examples of how these environments can be enhanced to support children.
- Consider how and when to interact with children within outdoor spaces.

Introduction

What do we know about how outdoor environments impact on young children's speech and language development? The short answer to this is... not a lot!!! This is a topic that is very rarely discussed in literature, and this chapter will therefore provide you with a perspective that is only just entering the research arena. A recent systematic review of the literature exploring this area found only 12 articles that explored speech and language development for young children within natural environments, and of those 12 articles, only four of them set out to explore this area; the rest discussed it retrospectively (Richardson et al., 2023). This indicates that this is an area that is under-researched and worthy of further discussion.

Bronfenbrenner (1979) recognised the importance of environment for children's development, and it has subsequently been acknowledged that young children's development differs dependant on the environment within which they are situated

(Hughes, 2010). This can also be said for speech and language development (Neaum, 2012). It has been established that both the environment and the interactions that occur within that environment are crucial elements that impact upon a child's development (Sutterby and Frost, 2006). We also know that children do not always learn in the same way. Some children prefer being in the outdoors and are more likely to learn and develop outside in a way that they would do not to indoors. This chapter will therefore consider how you can use nature and the outdoors to the benefit of young children and their speech and language development.

What can different outdoor environments offer children with regards to speech and language development?

The section that follows will consider how different environments can influence speech and language development.

Outdoor classrooms and playgrounds

When we think about outdoor classrooms within English Early Childhood contexts, we perhaps think of an extension of the indoor learning environment (Isaacs, 2012). The outdoor classroom quite often replicates the type of learning experiences that are provided within the indoor classroom and are planned and managed as such (Isaacs, 2012). The indoor and outdoor classrooms are often operated on a free-flow basis, meaning children can move freely from one environment to the other as they choose and can play and learn where suits them best.

The benefits of outdoor play are historically documented as being improvements on physical development (BERA/TACTYC, 2014), creativity (Sutterby and Frost, 2006) and social development (Waite and Pratt, 2013). However, more recently, there has begun a movement that has begun to recognise that outdoor spaces can also benefit speech and language development (Hackett et al., 2021; Richardson and Murray, 2016).

In addition to the outdoor classroom provision, schools in the United Kingdom also tend to provide space in which children can utilise gross motor skills: running, skipping, jumping, such as a playground or school field. These areas are generally accessed during break times or for physical education. Break times give children chance to 'let off steam' and generally have no learning intentions or structured provision of experience, invariably with no resources even provided it is solely an opportunity for children to have a break from learning. A playground environment, traditionally a large area of concreted space, again tends to benefit children beyond the expected physical development. The equipment provided within a playground provides an interesting contrast of benefits for children (Hughes, 2010). It has been found that new-style playgrounds, that schools in England have begun to install within their grounds for lunchtime and break-time play, tend to include structures for climbing and crawling through. It was discovered that more than half of play experiences around this kind of playground equipment were focused on social interaction, and around one quarter of play experiences were role-play based (Boyatzis, 1987). It could be argued therefore that this type of play equipment brings children together, in a social situation, and as a result enhances language development in an indirect manner. We will consider this further in the section that follows.

Natural environments and forest schools

Forest schools have become an increasingly popular addition to Early Years settings throughout the United Kingdom, after being introduced to the country from Sweden in the 1960s (Slade et al., 2013). Wellings (2012, p. 9) defines a forest school as 'a natural wooded environment to support the development of a relationship between the learner and the natural world'. Forest schools have continued to build on the pioneering work of Macmillan (1919) who highlighted the importance of natural outdoor play for children to be able to improve developmentally and improve overall health and well-being. Pretty et al. (2009) allege that, in addition to the well-documented physical benefits, the advantages of natural environments are that children are able to develop a deeper knowledge and understanding of their environment, develop socially and enhance behaviour strategies. It is also widely documented that self-esteem levels are enhanced by having access to a natural environment (Richardson, 2014). Again, as discussed above, it could be argued that each of these areas of development is intrinsically linked to speech and language development.

Research that specifically discusses speech and language development within natural environments talks of how the desire to communicate is enhanced when being in this environment (French, 2004), with children showing more enthusiasm in their language and wanting to talk more than they would when in an indoor environment. In addition to this, natural environments have been shown to increase children's vocabulary – giving them exposure to words that are context specific (Moffatt, 2016). After all, how much easier is it to learn about something and remember it when you have been able to see it and touch it in a real-world experience? And by expanding on their vocabulary, it enables children to talk more about their emotions (Miller, 2007), what they have learnt (Streelasky, 2019) and their experiences (Moffatt, 2016).

Children speak differently when they are in different environments (Richardson, 2014; Richardson and Murray, 2016). Research has found that when children are playing and learning within a natural environment, they use a greater number of verbs, more exclamation and richer lexical diversity. As we progress through this chapter, we will explore this further and think about what it is in these different environments that encourages communication and language.

When we think, as we have above, about how language development is intrinsically linked to all other areas of development, then it could be reasoned that if we are aiding one particular area of development, then it follows that other areas of development benefit also. Spend some time now reflecting on the below to consider how this manifests itself.

REFLECTION 4.1

Consider how the following areas of development impact on communication and language.

How could you support communication and language indirectly?

Consider the outdoors and the points raised in the section above:

Area of development	Impact that this may have on communication and language development	How you could encourage communication and language via this area of development
Physical development		
Social development		
Emotional development		
Cognitive development		

Table 4.1 How do areas of development impact on speech and language?

What elements within an outdoor environment prompt language learning and vocabulary

Taking the above points into consideration and realising that outdoor environments are beneficial for speech and language development, we therefore need to consider what needs to be within that environment to achieve the greatest impact. What is it about the outdoors that supports and encourages communication?

Comparing the outdoors to indoors, it could be said that children have a greater element of autonomy and freedom when outside, which could lead to a greater level of engagement with language. Outdoor environments may have fewer rules and boundaries. Sutterby and Frost (2006) acknowledge that when children play in an outdoor environment, compared with indoors, their play is messier, louder, less likely to be influenced by an adult, and as such leads to a deeper level of experimentation and exploration. It could be argued that this too could be beneficial to language development. It is recognised that some children can feel restricted

(Neaum, 2012) by the close supervision of adults. When playing indoors, it is usual to see observations underway, with an adult sporting a tablet or a clipboard and documenting the child's learning. This can result in them feeling pressurised into responding to questions in the correct manner, and consequently, it may be reasonable to assume that the greater independence and freedom within the outdoors could result in children flourishing.

REFLECTION 4.2

- *What do you think needs to be in an outdoor environment to promote communication and language?*
- *Does the environment need to include different things in it compared to the indoor environment?*
- *Do adults need to interact with children differently when they are outdoors?*

Once you have answered the questions above and considered your own viewpoint on this, read the case study below:

CASE STUDY 4.1 TEACH OUTDOORS

As a former primary teacher and founder of Teach Outdoors, Jo Clanfield has a keen interest in taking education beyond the classroom walls and is a leading advocate for outdoor learning. With experience in empowering educators nation-wide, Jo's expertise lies in harnessing the potential of outdoor environments for effective teaching and learning. She tells us:

> As an advisor in outdoor learning, I have personally witnessed the positive effects that outdoor environments have on communication and language development. I became aware of this when I observed a child in a Reception class who often seemed overwhelmed and disengaged indoors, but showed enthusiasm and engagement when given the opportunity to go outside. One particular day stands out in my memory, when we were building dens for the Three Little Pigs and acting out the story. To everyone's surprise, the boy started reciting the famous phrase, "I'll huff and I'll puff and I'll blow your house down," and actively joined in conversations with his peers, explaining the features of the den and finding natural objects to represent them. This transformation in his interaction was a breakthrough moment for the adults who had never seen him engage in this way before.

So, in the case study above, what was it in the outdoor environment that prompted that little boy to find his voice and share his learning with his peers? Perhaps the quote from Flannigan and Dietze below goes some way to explaining what is happening with him and why children often behave differently in different environments:

> *The outdoor environment provides a rich context that supports children in developing language and communication skills. A peaceful area surrounded by nature and free of background noise can motivate children to express themselves. Children can use their voice in a variety of ways, including pitches and volumes, without the usual constraints imposed in the indoor environments. The addition of loose parts in an outdoor environment provides further language development through the use of unfamiliar objects, new experiences, and the array of play possibilities.*
>
> (Flannigan and Dietze, 2017, p. 57)

The section that follows will therefore begin to explore further how these outdoor environments can be used to support children's speech and language development, using what we have learned throughout this chapter so far.

Practical examples of how these environments can be enhanced to support children

On the basis that outdoor and natural environments can benefit children with regards to their communication and language skills, it therefore is imperative that we give children the access to the outdoor spaces that they need. And once they are in those spaces, we need to ensure that the environment is set up in a way that will promote speech and language, a communication-friendly environment, as well as ensuring that the interactions are supportive and nurturing. So firstly, what do we mean by a communication-friendly environment? Jarman (2013) states that we need to use the environment and fulfil the potential of children by using our knowledge of how they develop to set the scene in a way that fosters well-being and high levels of engagement. A communication-friendly environment then is one in which children have the desire to express themselves. An environment that makes them feel comfortable and nurtured but at the same time allows them to be stimulated and excited by what is around them. Some of the aspects to consider to create this within an outdoor space will be discussed further below.

Provocations

Aspects that promote awe and wonder with children, provocations, are often considered to be extremely useful to prompt vocabulary learning within the outdoors. It is asserted that the need exists, within environments, for provocations to promote the 'unexpected' (Strong-Wilson and Ellis, 2007, p. 42). Cadwell (2003) believes these provocations bring the environment an element of excitement, and it makes the environment feel 'electric and alive' (Cadwell, 2003, p. 118). It could be said that this 'unexpected' is the driving force for awe and wonder in young children and therefore prompts enthusiasm and enhances the spoken word. These objects not only prompt interest but enhance lexical richness (Jarvis, 2013) both within the setting and when children expand on their experiences within the home environment. Provocations can exist within any environment but tend to be more naturally occurring within the outdoor environment. That said, it is also possible to enhance these naturally occurring elements and influence the children's experiences as required.

CASE STUDY 4.2 PROMOTING LANGUAGE IN THE OUTDOORS

When asked about what she thinks makes a difference in the outdoors, Jo Clanfield, who talked to us above about the differences she had noted in her practice in the case study above, says:

> I have witnessed various strategies being implemented in outdoor settings to promote conversations, such as floating messages in bottles on ponds, leaving intriguing objects like large keys for children to discover, and even burying old tin boxes containing an object of interest in the ground as stimuli for activities. It is also important to note that natural environments often offer excellent opportunities for spontaneous discussions, such as encountering a colourful, hairy caterpillar. Seizing these moments and engaging in dialogue about the experiences naturally sparks curiosity and leads to meaningful conversations. The opportunities for exploration and thought-provoking prompts that outdoor environments provide serve as excellent springboards for conversations and the introduction of new language.

Opportunities for collaboration

It is recognised that for children's speech and language to be enhanced, children need to work, and interact, with others, aligning with the interactionist approach to speech and language development (Tomasello, 2003). There is a need for the environment and resources to facilitate this collaboration, but not necessarily in the traditional sense, with planning and purchasing, but also having resources that are unplanned and naturally occurring. It is therefore essential that any environment for play and learning provides the opportunity for collaboration. When we think of outdoor play and learning spaces, there are many opportunities for children to play together, and if the environment is set up in such a way that allows this, then this is likely to be so, but it may be that elements do need to be added to enhance this further and loose parts, or transportable elements are often ideal in this situation.

Loose parts/transportable resources

Transportable, open-ended resources are necessary within an environment to promote speech and language development. By providing resources with no predetermined purpose, that can be moved between environments, it has been found that this can promote imagination and exploration. Whitebread et al. (2015) believe that for playful learning to occur, there is a need for this open-ended play. It is suggested that these resources are likely to be more freely available within a natural outdoor environment as these resources are generally naturally occurring (Wellings, 2012) and therefore looser in essence. Within an outdoor classroom-type space, more of a concerted effort is required to place loose parts into the environment. Some suggestions of loose parts/transportable resources that can be placed within an environment are things such as:

- Planks.
- Milk crates.
- Tyres.
- Bricks.
- Rocks/pebbles.
- Sheets/tarpaulin.
- Cones/leaves/conkers/seed pods.
- Logs.
- Shells.
- Canes.

It could be suggested that children's imaginations are fostered within a natural outdoor environment as they do not have such a variety of resources available to them as they do when indoors, and those resources that are available are open ended so have no fixed purpose. This creates imaginary play and encourages children to express themselves more, hence expanding vocabulary and lexical richness (Sutterby and Frost, 2006).

Quiet areas

It is noted that children require quiet areas in which to process thought and engage in meaningful dialogue (Whitebread et al., 2015); it is suggested that outdoors environments are more likely to provide this opportunity. The provision of space is likely to be greater in the outdoors compared to inside, and it is likely that it is the way that this space is utilised that can impact on the provision of the quiet areas. It could be that it is necessary to purposely provide some space where children can take themselves off and have time to process and have a time of quiet, by constructing dens, mazes and seated areas tucked away. It is argued that this is a contributory factor to the quality of children's utterances and is therefore an element that requires attention from practitioners. Reed (2012, p. 17) states that 'favourable conditions' are required within a quality environment to assist with listening and speaking. It is therefore suggested that these 'favourable conditions' should include areas where children can be quiet, where they can process their thoughts and can listen to others with ease. Meaningful dialogue is recognised as being essential (Whitebread et al., 2015), and it is asserted that this quiet space is essential for this meaningful dialogue to take place effectively. At the same time as saying this though, it is also recognised that this does not necessarily need to be restricted to a specific area of the environment. As long as children have the space and time to process, to get away from the busyness of the environment, then this can give them the opportunity to gain a sense of enclosure and safety, aiding the developmental process.

The need for interaction

Although so far this chapter has discussed the use of the outdoor environment to promote speech and language development, we cannot ignore the need for interactions within these environments. We know that children learn best, while being supported by others and by the environment (Vygotsky, 1962). We also know that children learn best when supported by quality interactions (Sylva et al., 2004), so it is imperative that we interact with children in whichever environment they choose to play and learn. Fisher (2016) discusses the tension that can often arise between 'interacting or interfering?' – should we, as professionals, step in to encourage development when children are engaged in their play? Consider the situation below and reflect on the questions posed.

REFLECTION 4.3

A group of children are immersed in playing in the outdoor space. They are playing in the sand pit and are busy constructing a bridge so that their imaginary dogs can get across the sand without getting their paws dirty.

- *How do you interact without interfering and interrupting the flow of their play?*
- *How can you support their play and their vocabulary without interrupting and interfering?*
- *What is the best use of language in this situation?*

What we need to avoid within the outdoors is the 'stand and supervise' approach. We have shown throughout this chapter that the outdoors is so much more than just a space for letting off steam and children therefore need the scaffolding support of the more knowledgeable other (Vygotsky, 1962) in order to enhance their learning opportunities. Skilful practitioners are needed to encourage exploration, risk taking, collaboration and imagination in a way that develops the breadth of vocabulary, pragmatics (the social rules of language) and expression. Early Education (2021, p. 19) states that 'children's language is enriched and enhanced by back-and-forth exchanges with practitioners who respect and respond to children's conversation'. This reciprocity is a delicate balancing act. Fisher (2016) maintains that when deciding how to interact with children, adults should firstly decide who is leading the learning. If a child is leading the learning, then Fisher argues that adults should 'resist any temptation to hijack that learning for their own purposes' (2016, p. 97), something that we can often see happen in practice. Imagine as an adult that you were deeply engaged in something and somebody came over to you and said 'what are you doing? What colour is that object? How many of those do you have? Can you share with your friends...' How frustrating would that be? We would think it disrespectful and rude, and yet we do that to children regularly. What children need therefore are respectful and intuitive adults who know when to interact and when to interfere. This can take time and confidence as a practitioner to develop this skill.

What can occur in outdoor spaces is that children end up playing a distance away from adults and therefore do not end up having as much interaction as they would in more enclosed spaces (Richardson et al., 2023). As a result, this can mean that children do not get the same level of interaction as they would indoors. Adults therefore need to proactively engage with children to ensure that they are supported accordingly. So how do we do this?

CASE STUDY 4.3 SELF-REFLECTION WITHIN A FOREST SCHOOL

Tracy a nursery setting manager explains how she encourages this within her setting.

> The children in our setting spend a lot of time outdoors. We are lucky enough to have a forest school on our site and they therefore spend a great deal of time in the woods, playing and learning in nature. I realised that the practitioners were interacting differently with the children when in this space – and not necessarily in a good way. They held back more, did not initiate conversations as often and generally were not so engaged. That made me question how we could improve this and support children's exploration of language more. On one occasion I videoed the session, with everyone's knowledge obviously, and we watched the video back as a team. The practitioners noted themselves that there were lots of missed opportunities for meaningful interactions. We therefore decided to take some positive action and did the following:

(Continued)

(Continued)

- *Approached children where they were playing but sat a little way away, fiddling with something nearby, until inevitably they engaged with us and invited us into their play. The key here was not to interrupt but be near so that they remembered we were there and engaged with us when they were ready.*
- *Sat a distance away but started to play with something very interesting and make interested noises. Often the children would approach and ask what we were doing/what we had found, and conversation would flow readily.*
- *Never ask direct closed questions – instead say things such as 'I wonder what would happen if....' 'I'm not sure what is happening here....' to promote extended vocabulary and conversation.*

When we reflected on the effectiveness of this approach, we found that this was much more successful from a speech and language perspective. We continue to reflect and tweak our practice, but the steps above have definitely seen a positive impact.

CHAPTER SUMMARY

When considering your pedagogical approach to supporting speech and language within the outdoors, this chapter has highlighted the need for consideration to be given to both the environment and the interactions that occur within that environment. The outdoors should not be an extension of the inside environment but, due to the benefits that the outdoors can afford, should be treated as a separate entity and given special consideration. It is recognised that our individual pedagogy comes from our own beliefs of child development, our own experiences of childhood and our sociocultural context. Our pedagogical approach to the outdoors is therefore very much individualised. This chapter will have gone some way to allow you to reflect on what is important to you when considering how you want to practice with children in outdoor spaces, and what you can do to assist them in the important area of speech and language development. It is likely that this reflection is an ongoing process, and it may be that you want to return to this chapter periodically to remind you of aspects that can aid your practice and therefore support the children in your care accordingly.

KEY QUESTIONS

Now that you have engaged in the content of this chapter, consider the questions below:

- *In what way could you use what you have learnt in this chapter to enhance your practice and develop your pedagogical approach?*
- *How could you enhance young children's communication and language by using the outdoor environment?*
- *How could you share what you have learnt with parents or carers so that they can consider where they take their children to play, and what they do with them when they are playing?*

Further reading and resources

Birth 2 Five Matters – Available from: https://birthto5matters.org.uk/wp-content/uploads/2021/04/Birthto5Matters-download.pdf

Birth 2 Five Matters: Guidance for the sector, by the sector is a document that has been written by a range of experts to give an alternative view to Early Years Foundation Stage curriculum. There is a section within the guidance on enabling environments and also on communication and language development so can assist your thinking accordingly.

Elizabeth Jarman is the founder of The Communication Friendly Spaces Approach, and her website and publications give lots of practical ideas on how to create communication rich environments and also spaces that are welcoming and nurturing: https://elizabethjarman.com/

5 GLOBAL PERSPECTIVES ON COMMUNICATION IN THE OUTDOORS

KATARINA DOLGAN AND TANYA RICHARDSON

THIS CHAPTER

By actively reading this chapter and engaging with the material, you will be able to:

- Consider how nature and forest schools can support communication and language development.
- Compare and contrast practitioner experiences of supporting language in nature in several countries.
- Develop language stimulating strategies to help to support children with their speech, language and communication beyond the classroom.

Introduction

We know that children learn and develop differently dependant on the culture and society in which they live and are brought up, and the same applies for language development. We can consider Bronfenbrenner's ecological model when thinking about this (see Figure 1.1). The model shows us that what is going on around the child, both directly and indirectly, impacts on their growth and development.

Language development is certainly influenced by the culture in which the child develops. Consider, for example, how different parts of the country where you are living say different things. Across the same country, there are often different accents, different dialects and different vocabulary used. What, for example, do you call the bread that you put a burger in? In parts of the United Kingdom, this can be called a roll, a bap, a cob, a barmcake, a bun, a batch or something else entirely! What a child calls this item therefore will be heavily influenced by the people around them, where those people are situated and the political and historical context which they are in.

So, if we consider how these differences impact on language development, and then add into the mix the differences in the way that outdoor play is promoted and encouraged, this can add a whole extra dimension to how we consider speech and language development. This chapter will therefore allow you to explore different approaches to supporting language development within the outdoors, particularly focusing on forest schools and natural environments, and how different countries approach this.

How can nature and forest schools support communication and language development?

Chapter 4 discussed the importance of children being immersed in nature and how England has imported the forest school approach across settings throughout the country. It is recognised though that this approach throughout England operates on a kind of 'pick and mix' system – not always in the true forest school style but instead taking elements of the approach and adapting it depending on the situation and geographical location. In addition to this, beach schools have begun to be a popular addition to some settings, offering children the opportunity to 'harness the magic of the ocean and the charm of coastal environments to inspire curiosity, creativity, and a deep connection with nature' (Forest Schools Education, 2023). Research informs us that being within a natural environment enhances children's vocabulary (Richardson and Murray, 2016) in the following ways:

Verb usage

It has been found that when children are in the natural environment, they use more verbs – more 'doing' words – and it is likely to be that the more a child is doing, then the more they talk about what they are doing. It is known that there is a neurological link between movement and the use of voice (McGilchrist, 2009). If children are doing and moving more, this results in the ability to gesture, to point, to enable access to points of significant interest and to be engaged in more. This, in turn, can increase the potential for the extension of vocabulary, the use of more doing words and therefore enhance language development (Cunningham et al., 2023). This also works in reverse; Bedford et al. (2015) have indeed found some correlation indicating that reduced motor functions appeared to impact negatively upon the development of language. It is therefore important that we expose children to the kinds of environments that allow movement and allow them to 'do'.

Exclamations

Research shows that when children are within a natural environment, they use more exclamation words (such as 'oh', 'whooahhh', 'cool'), compared to when they are indoors. It is likely that this is due to the excitement and enjoyment that the children experience when in a forest school or natural space. When children play in the open space that natural environments tend to afford, they are more likely to be in smaller groups and therefore more likely to be able to express themselves without restriction. This acknowledges the work of Kitzinger (1995), who reports that the 'bystander effect' (p. 16) can impact upon a child's responses when in a large group, meaning they are more likely to become passive and conforming to their peer's behaviours. Bruce (2004) informs us that if children are playing in smaller groups, then they are 'more likely to develop a sensitive, caring and thoughtful approach with skilful communication and language' (p. 70).

Adjective usage

The richness of adjectives and the usage of these words has been found to be enhanced when children play in the natural environment, and the adjectives used when they are playing and learning in these spaces are very different in nature. Adjective usage in the natural environment has been found to be more descriptive (with words such as 'wriggly', 'sticky' and 'slimy' being used), which is likely to be because the natural space being more of a sensory experience. If you imagine being in an indoor space and consider what you can hear, smell and see, and then do the same imagining you are in a forest type environment, it is probable that you are imagining a much more sensory environment when metaphorically putting yourself into the natural space. If a child is in that environment in real life, then they will be engaging more of their senses, which in turn activates more areas of the brain and therefore leads that child to learn, process and remember more over time.

Although the points above indicate that children speak differently in different play spaces, and that the natural environment has been found to be beneficial for language development, this does come with a caveat. It is worth noting that this is not going to be the case for *every* child. Some children really do not like to be in the outdoors, they don't like to be cold or they don't like to get dirty. We still have to consider each child and their uniqueness – it is never a one-size-fits-all approach.

REFLECTION 5.1

Considering the points raised above about how children speak differently when in natural environments, observe a child you know and note how they communicate when in different spaces.

- *Do they use different language in different environments? If so, how does it differ?*
- *Are they more engaged in their play and learning outside?*
- *Are they playing in smaller groups?*
- *Are they talking more?*

Reflect on what you observe and how you could use this knowledge to further enhance the experiences that you provide for that child and their learning.

Early language development in nature

Even though nature is not mentioned in Bronfenbrenner's ecological model (Bronfenbrenner, 1979), which is described above, it most certainly has a significant influence on child growth and development. Numerous researchers have studied children's development in nature, recognising the importance of outdoor experiences for cognitive, emotional and physical development.

Nature does not only help children with regards to physical and emotional development; natural environments have a significant impact on language acquisition and communication skills as well. Wilson describes how nature-rich environments can provide opportunities for language learning (Wilson, 2018), and Richardson et al. (2023) outline the benefits that being in nature can have on language learning (discussed in Chapter 4). Although there is evidence that has come from the research and supporting literature that nature can be beneficial for young children's speech and language development, this does not always translate to practice within kindergartens and schools. When observing the pedagogical practice of outdoor learning across different European countries, we can see a big variation between practices.

International approaches to play and learning in natural environments

The points raised above have built on experiences within English forest schools and natural environments. As a comparison, we will take some time now to look at approaches to nature and forest school across other countries.

The section that follows will explore a project that was undertaken to compare practice across Slovenia, Germany and Sweden. Representatives from each of these countries participated in a European project for early language development in nature – ELaDiNa (Kokalj et al., 2023). When analysing the data from this research project, some significant common features of different approaches to early language development in nature were found in different countries.

The target participants all worked with children from three to seven years old, and the purpose of the project was to identify, highlight and utilise the possibilities and opportunities offered by learning in nature and thus improve the child's communication skills. The participants shared experiences and activities that were undertaken in their settings and how these aided speech and language development.

Participants in the project had the opportunities to try out different strategies, and the following case studies show us how the previous experience of participants, the environment that they come from and their personal approach to outdoor learning, can influence the selection of activities for children to learn language in nature.

CASE STUDY 5.1 MAJA

When Maja, a first grade primary school teacher in Slovenia, was asked about how she used language strategies in nature, she said:

> Before going out with my pupils I carefully read and selected objectives from the syllabus, connected to the outdoor learning. Then I chose which strategy I will be focused on. According to them I started to plan different activities for pupils to achieve the objectives and usage of strategies as well. I prepared various didactic material and sent a notice to parents when, where and what will we do, when we will go out in the woods.
>
> On the day, when we went out, I had a detailed conversation with pupils about the activities, about the rules and their behaviour in the woods. When we got there, pupils knew exactly what to do and they started to do activities usually in small groups. That gave me the opportunity to try out different strategies, especially on how to "focus on quiet children". I realised that I have more time to talk and to be focused on the individuals, if I plan the activities for pupils well and they know exactly what to do, when we come into the woods. Almost all members of groups did all the activities successfully. When we came back to the classroom, we checked their answers on their working sheets and most of them were right. We ended our day in woods with self-evaluation regarding to new gained knowledge and their feelings during the activities. My pupils described the day spent in the woods as one of their best days in school. We all agreed that we should do that more often.
>
> But to organise that kind of day with six-year-old children ... Well, that is quite a challenge! I would go out with them more often because obviously they learn more and feel better, but I'm so afraid that something might happen to someone. You cannot be careful enough with those kinds of activities. That is why we have so many rules and obligations and we agree about them with pupils even before we go out. For me structured outdoor lessons mean more taking control of situations out there and consequently less options for someone to get hurt.

When the research project analysed other examples of Slovenian teachers, it was noted that a similar structure and very well-organised activities were planned, with lots of supporting didactic material. And most of them gave the same reason for approaching the outdoor learning in a specific way; safety first.

On the other hand, there was a different approach to the language development in nature with German kindergarten teachers. It was noted that they do not tend to plan everything in advance as much as their Slovenian colleges do. They tended to be much more intuitive, and it seems as though they follow the child's lead and establish joint attention as a matter of course. Children particularly enjoy a conversation when the common focus of attention is on an object or topic that has meaning for a child. To establish this situation, a dialogue partner should hold back their own ideas and must fully engage with the child's interests. Fisher (2016, p. 76) explains that 'in order to tune in to the child, the practitioner must be fascinated by children'. And although this may appear obvious, this level of interaction requires the pedagogue to give the child their whole focus and attention, which can often be difficult in busy environments.

CASE STUDY 5.2 LISA-MARIE

Lisa-Marie, a kindergarten teacher from Germany, explains how she observes and develops this fascination, in order to engage with children and to use nature to support speech and language.

When I go out with children, I like to give them time and space for playing on their own. Observing them engaging in their free unstructured game gives me an opportunity to see, how they think, what they like, what is the point of their interest... And at the same time, I get an insight into their social contacts and level of communication skills. The basic activities like playing with mud or jumping in puddles are perfect for me to participate in their game. A relaxed atmosphere and a safe and stimulating learning environment increase the children's urge to share their feelings, their fears, the excitement, everything that is going on inside of them and around them with everyone around, regardless of if this is me or one of their friends. I just follow their lead and try to fit in as much as I can.

For someone, who would observe these activities and would not be aware of the significant impact of them on the communication skills development of children, they might seem ridiculous or even a waste of time. But as soon as a teacher experiences how it is to be included in the children's circle, to really participate in their game as an equal member of the group, it gives them an insight into a child's thinking and opportunity to discover and increase their communication skills.

That is the main reason why we sometimes go out and do whatever children would like to do. And it does not matter if the sun is shining, or the rain is falling. Their suggestions are the ones that count the most. And we try to fulfil them as much as it is possible. This is the time for fun and joy but at the same time we learn so much from each other. We all really enjoy the time spent outside.

Analysing the two approaches to early language development in nature outlined above, from Slovenia and Germany, it shows us that these two versions are polar opposites in their pedagogical approach. It is also pertinent to note that although these are polar opposites, one approach is not necessarily better than the other, producing better results than the other, but both are relevant to the context and the culture in which they are situated. When considering how you would like to practice with young children, it is worth thinking about which end of the spectrum you feel is more suitable to your context, or if maybe you choose your own version between those two.

The approach adopted by teachers from Sweden gives us another completely different perspective. Swedish teachers, in general, consider that outdoor learning has a whole new meaning in their everyday school life. They don't plan it as much as their colleagues from the other two countries do mostly because it is their daily routine. They don't go out just few times per month; they go out every day. They say that each day is a perfect day for an outdoor learning. This is, in part, due to the tradition of outdoor learning in Sweden and the fact that this has the biggest impact on the organisation and equipment of schools. Most of the classrooms in Sweden's schools and kindergartens have direct access to the outdoor learning spaces or outdoor classrooms. As such, there is no need to plan special days or lessons for children to learn about nature within nature. And if they need to learn how to grow lettuce, for example, they don't watch a video or read about that. Instead, they go outside, sow the seeds, take good care of them, watch them grow and learn what they need for their growth. They learn that through their own experience.

CASE STUDY 5.3 THINA

Thina, a pedagogue from Sweden, explains how she uses outdoor spaces in her teaching:

> Since I started to teach, outdoor learning was part of my practice. It was something I grew up with and if I look back now, I can say that I have learned the most and been most efficient when I was surrounded with nature. We are really very connected with it in Sweden. Maybe this is the main reason why I go out with my pupils so often.
>
> We have lots of open space areas around our school where children can play, observe or get to know better basic processes that take place in nature. On lots of Saturdays also their parents join us, and they help with the arrangement of the external surrounding of our school. Every child in my classroom has their own space to store the basic equipment for going out in any kind of weather and circumstances. And everyone is responsible to take care for their own stuff.

At the beginning of the school year, we set the rules about going out and children are used to them. They follow them through the whole school year. They also know, that should they have an urge for a quick breath of fresh air or some kind of movement, they do not need special permission to go out on the yard of our classroom. By the way, each of our classrooms in our school has its own outdoor space.

When we all go out, we are mainly focused on discovering new things, observing what is new outside and try to find as many answers as we can for the questions we have set in classroom. Children are used to working in pairs or groups, others would rather stay on their own. It is up to them. Working in pairs or groups gives them an opportunity to develop social and communication skills. They follow the same goal to finish a task and they learn quite fast that success of the group depends on every single member of the group. So, I have many opportunities to have a conversation with every single pupil in my classroom.

When Swedish teachers were asked which language stimulating strategy they found most useful in nature, they explained that 'naming unknown words frequently' was the most widely used approach. Children appear to work well together, and collaboration is effective in the discovery of new skills, talents and vocabulary. Expanding vocabulary is a key skill when developing speech and language abilities. Words and their meanings must be securely stored in a mental lexicon so they can be recalled in any required situation. Secure memorisation is supported when dialogue partners allow intensive exploration with all their senses and linguistically accompany this process. Many repetitions in different contexts are helpful for memorising a new or unfamiliar word (Kokalj et al., 2023).

The conclusion that can be drawn from the above case studies and from the ELaDiNa project is that there is a recognition that outdoor learning encompasses all that children do, see, hear or feel in their outdoor spaces. It is therefore important to consider:

- experiences that practitioners create and plan for;
- spontaneous activities that children initiate;
- naturally occurring cyclical opportunities linked to the seasons, weather and nature.

The project also highlighted that, when choosing a rich outdoor learning environment, teachers should consider whether it offers opportunities:

- for children to handle natural materials such as: stones, branches, water, mud, etc.;
- for the outdoors to become a classroom, a laboratory, a gym, a playroom, a workshop, a place for exploration, a place for calm, a place for participation (e.g. teamwork) (Kokalj and Novak, 2023).

Although all participants in the project received the same input initially by way of a training session, it was noted that there were some major differences between the approaches of participants from different countries. The case studies above could indicate that Slovenian teachers are more structured when it comes to the outdoor activities, they give lots of instructions to their children, all the activities are target-oriented and they very much follow goals from the syllabus. In contrast, their German colleagues are more into 'trust the process approach', which means that they take their children out and sometimes just observe what children are doing, and then they follow their lead. For Sweden participants, outdoor learning is almost part of their everyday life. From an outsider's perspective, it might seem that they do not need to put lots of effort to organise activities in nature for children. It all looks so natural and easy for them, like everything runs smoothly without a huge effort. It could be that this is due to outdoor learning in Sweden having such a long tradition, that this becomes entrenched in their practice in this way.

A hypothetical example

As the case studies above show, there are numerous considerations for choosing an appropriate environment, numerous opportunities within natural environments that can evoke language-stimulating situations and differences in the way that the adults plan activities and interact when in the environment itself. However, to turn these opportunities into real language-learning moments for children, attentive adults are needed to recognise these situations, decide on an appropriate one and accompany them linguistically in a supportive way. Let's take, for example, a scenario when children are taken into the woods. Even if they only walk through it, there are so many unpredictable situations when they might need to communicate, to use different words, especially adjectives, if they want to describe everything that they feel or experience. Just imagine the situation where children are given a task to build a shelter for an animal that lives in a forest, and they need to do that in pairs. These kinds of activities really offer opportunities for children to communicate, collaborate, develop their creativity and use their imagination. For the early development of communication skills, it is also important that they need to describe and explain how the chosen animal would live there. They may need the support from adults in developing the vocabulary to assist with this.

Language stimulating strategies to help to support children with speech, language and communication beyond the classroom

We therefore also need to understand that it is not activities alone that are language-stimulating. Only sensitive, responsive dialogue during and/or after activities turns them into successful language-learning opportunities for children. In their language acquisition process, children need appropriate dialogue partners who are familiar with the art of language stimulation, modelling techniques and other language-stimulating strategies and who react sensitively and contingently to children's verbal or non-verbal utterances. Such shaping and support of conversation have a decisive impact on whether such activities have a beneficial effect on children's language acquisition (Saxton, 2017).

Following the comparative and collaborative approach of the ELaDiNa project discussed above (Kokalj and Novak, 2023), numerous strategies and communicative considerations were devised and considered to assist with the stimulation of language development. The following language-stimulating strategies are recommended for use within nature:

- Adopt a fundamental language-supportive attitude
    - Move down to the child's eye level.
    - Maintain eye contact.
    - Pay full attention to the child.
    - Assume a facing posture.
    - Use affirmative facial expressions.
    - Listen and let the child speak.
    - Ask questions with interest.
    - Radiate the joy of communication.
- Follow your child's lead – establish joint attention
    - Observe, wait, listen.
    - Perceive and focus on the child's interests.
    - Give up one's own leadership and follow the child.
- Parallel talk and self-talk
    - Accompanying the child's actions with language.
    - Speak about your own actions.
    - Use this strategy, especially when the child is attentive.
- Confirm, repeat and expand the child's utterances
    - First, find words to confirm a child's utterances and repeat what has been said in the sense of active listening.
    - Add one more piece of information or expand it with a limited/manageable number of new considerations.
    - When making additional comments, pick up on a topic and interest of a child.

- Corrective feedback
  - Repeat utterances with correct pronunciation and grammar.
  - Repeat incomplete sentences completely.
  - Use this strategy repeatedly but sensitively.
- Name unknown words frequently
  - Repeat new, unknown words frequently and meaningfully in different contexts.
- Use appropriate and rich language
  - Use well-formulated, detailed language.
  - Avoid abbreviated statements.
  - Use a maximum strategy of verbalisation instead of a minimal strategy.
- Turn-taking – pay attention to reciprocity in dialogue
  - Pay attention to reciprocity in dialogue.
  - Create several changes of speaker.
  - Pay attention to enabling a balanced proportion of speech or increase the children's share of speech.
  - If necessary, take a back seat more often.
- Focus on quiet children
  - Recognise which children are sociable and communicative and which are not.
  - Take initiative and actively seek contact with quiet children.
- Avoid imperatives
  - Encourage children to think for themselves instead of issuing prohibitions.
  - Allow a child to come up with their own ideas and to act independently; discuss consequences with each other.
- Asking questions
  - Use questions in a measured way because they are not stimulating for all children.
  - Ask fewer questions and accompany children more linguistically.
  - Ask open rather than closed questions.
  - Use alternative questions for insecure children.

(Kokalj et al., 2023)

Although these language-stimulating strategies have been devised with natural environments in mind, it is argued that these will be equally as effective in any play and learning environment, and these strategies should provide opportunities for professional reflection wherever the child is engaged with others.

REFLECTION 5.2

Taking the above comparative case studies into account, take some time to consider what elements of the above practice can assist young children's speech and language development (you might want to refer back to Chapter 4 here to remind yourself about some aspects in the outdoors that are known to help language development).

- *What parts of the practice discussed above do you think could be used in the context that you work in with children?*
- *What aspects wouldn't work so well?*
- *Why do you think this is the case?*

CHAPTER SUMMARY

This chapter has considered the sociocultural context in which a child is situated and the impact that this can have on speech and language learning within outdoor natural environments. It has illustrated through case studies drawn from various European countries that there is not a 'one-size-fits-all' approach, and that what happens within an environment is just as important as the environment itself. It has hopefully given you opportunity to reflect on how you can use nature within your own practice to support language and has given some suggestions of strategies that you can use both inside and outdoors to encourage children to develop accordingly.

KEY QUESTIONS

Consider the language stimulating strategies outlined in this chapter:

- *What particular strategy could you see as being useful for you to work on?*
- *Could you perhaps pick one or two and try out the strategies over a period of time to see what impact they made?*

(Continued)

(Continued)

Think about the cultures that the children that you work with come from.

- *Have the differences in their environments impacted on how they speak and communicate?*
- *What can you do to support ALL children, regardless of cultural background, and how can you use these differences to the children's advantage?*

Further reading and resources

Kokalj, I. et al. (2023). ELaDiNa Practical Handbook [online] Available from: https://www.csod.si/uploads/file/PROJEKTI/ELaDiNa/Prakticni%20prirocnik_ELaDiNa_ANG_2023_zaSplet.pdf [accessed 30/10/23].

The practical handbook that was produced as a result of the European project provides a wealth of examples, ideas and approaches for assisting young children's language development in nature.

6 WORKING TOGETHER WITH PARENTS

JULIE KENT AND LAURA SANDERS

THIS CHAPTER

By actively reading this chapter and engaging with the material, you will be able to:

- Explore elements of professional practice in relation to good communication practice across the setting with children and families.
- Recognise the significance of working with parents and families in understanding children's speech, language and communication (SLC). ('Parents' is used throughout as shorthand to represent parents and carers.)
- Use examples from practice-based research to challenge your approaches to working together to support children's SLC in your own setting.
- Gain insights into the sensitivities of working with children and families in the area of SLC.

Introduction

Learning from research shows us that parents are key to their young children's development and learning, and that supporting parents as educators supports children's later academic achievement (Hannon et al., 2020; Nutbrown et al., 2022). Dating back to the 1990 Rumbold report into nursery provision in the United Kingdom, 'Starting with Quality' (DfE, 1990), there has been a recognition of the central importance of working with parents. The report identified a number of key areas where Early Years (EY) practitioners can work most effectively with parents.

> *What is needed is for educators to **be able and willing to explain to parents** how the experiences offered to children contribute to their learning, and to **describe how their children are progressing**. They need to **be prepared to share responsibility** with parents. This places considerable demands upon the educators they need to be **ready to spend time** on it, and to **exercise sensitivity;** they also need to have enough **confidence to invite parents to share in their children's***

> ***education**. They must ensure that they have the **necessary skills to work effectively with parents**.*
>
> (DfE, 1990, p. 13)

This excerpt, still highly relevant in today's Early Childhood environment, captures several aspects of good practice in this area, including confidence in one's own knowledge and skills but also a mindset of sharing responsibility for children's learning with parents and a willingness to spend time on building a relationship where knowledge is exchanged with a sensitive approach between the setting and the home. The underpinning suggestion is of a reciprocal, respectful relationship, and this is particularly important in the sensitive and significant area of children's SLC where it is possible to make judgements or assumptions about parental levels of involvement, language use and communication if a shared approach is not taken. Relational working, based in strong communication practice, should be at the heart of our work with children and families in Early Childhood, and this will be explored in the rest of this chapter.

Some research perspectives

It is clearly identified in research that parental language input is one of the strongest predictors of positive language outcomes for the child. A research study which involved parent coaching in effective early communication strategies evidenced that early parental language use with the child significantly improved child language growth (Ferjan-Ramirez et al., 2020).

Global research-informed perspectives also support EY practitioners to consider how the family and home learning environment are viewed. Adams and Myran's 2022 research recognises the relationship between parental and community engagement and children's learning outcomes through the creation of high-quality early childhood provision. Parents described how their experiences of interactions with early childhood leaders provided limited communication opportunities, lack of 'space' for information-sharing and difficulty developing positive relationships. Parents in this research described how much they valued being recognised as 'credible knowers' (p. 73), that is, as experts in their own child with relevant information to share.

International research into examples of good practice approaches shows that family-centred practice, based around two central parameters of relationships and participation, where family strengths are honoured, has a significant benefit for outcomes for the child and the family (Dunst and Espe-Sherwindt, 2016).

A systems perspective on communication relationships

Communication and language is a complex area of a child's early development which involves many interactions and experiences in the home, the early childhood education and care (ECEC) setting and the child's wider community. The systems perspective outlined in chapter one is a useful way of considering this area of development, and the Ecological Systems Theory (EST) (Bronfenbrenner, 2004) will be applied in this chapter as a theoretical framework in which to view the connections between a child's environments from the most intimate early relationships in the home, through early educational experiences and the influence of those societal systems which may support or influence children's C&L (Kent and Moran, 2019). The EST provides a useful model for exploring the relationships in the child's microsystem where SLC develops, with the child at the centre of a series of systems. This sociocultural theory recognises that human development, including SLC, occurs, not just within the individual but also in the context of the environment, time period, culture and societal structures in which they live.

The child's microsystem consists of the closest early relationships which the child has in their day-to-day lived experiences. This is also discussed in relation to grandparents in Chapter 7. In the earliest years of life, this is a space where child-sensitive communication approaches in the home and good practice in settings can have an early impact on children's skills in this area of development, potentially preventative of later or continuing difficulties without the need for specialist intervention. In researching the association between disadvantage and speech, language and communication needs (SLCN), research and interventions generally focus on the two central elements of the child's microsystem: the home learning environment (HLE) and the quality of EY provision. Consequently, alongside general setting-wide good communication practice, the essential aspect of connecting with the child's home and family is recognised. As part of this, the initial identification of actual or potential SLCN becomes a key part of a practitioner's role (Nicholson, 2020). Research has shown that higher levels of parental involvement at two years were associated with better learning outcomes at six years (Hayes and Berthelsen, 2020). Shared book reading is given as an example which supports children's later communication and language skills. Although the research findings showed that parents from lower socio-economic backgrounds were less engaged with these shared reading activities, Hayes and Berthelsen (2020) are careful in noting that families' needs and circumstances should be considered in a respectful and responsive way, something which we as EY practitioners need to hold in mind when working with families.

A supportive EY framework

As EY practitioners, using the familiar overarching principles of the Early Years Foundation Stage (EYFS) (DfE, 2024) is a useful way to consider this area of development, and this section will explore C&L using these principles:

- A unique child – your knowledge of each child in your care is essential, considering each one as an individual with different skills, abilities and challenges.

- Positive relationships – strong attachments are a platform for providing rich learning experiences in particular with regard to C&L development. The key-person role is central in building a strong communication relationship with each child and their family.
- Enabling environments – within the daily practice in creating and managing the environment, there are challenges involved in identifying and enabling a language-rich environment, both setting-wide and for each individual child and their parents.
- Learning and development – is underpinned by the characteristics of effective learning and teaching to support children as they learn and develop at different rates, and to support parents in partnership with the setting.

Using these principles will support you to start from what you know about the child and their family and be creative in developing core resources and relevant teaching approaches as you lead practice in working together with parents to support development in this prime area.

A unique child

In the EY, it is essential to recognise what experiences and knowledge the child already brings to the setting from their microsystem (see Figure 1) (Bronfenbrenner, 2004) and for practitioners to consider how a child's everyday life has already helped them to develop their communication skills. Responding to current societal and family structures in the exosystem (see Figure 1), it is evident that, alongside the family, the EY setting will increasingly be key to supporting this and other aspects of early child development. The Study of Early Education and Development (SEED) longitudinal study (DfE, 2020) is exploring the take-up of early education for two- to three-year-old children and is studying the associations between the amount of differing types of ECEC and child development, as well as associations between child development and aspects of the home environment. Findings from the report (2020) suggest that, on school entry, children who spent more hours from the age of two in formal ECEC did not develop language skills as effectively as those who had spent more time in informal childcare (such as with relatives and friends). These findings show a complex interplay between the home and setting environment and present a challenge to EY practitioners in ensuring that each child in their care is supported by people within their microsystem who not only have relevant training, knowledge and skills but who also know and understand the child as an individual.

From an EST perspective, the mesosystem is the space in which those parts of a child's microsystem interact in a two-way process to support the child at the centre (see Figure 1). By finding out what each child likes and what helps the child to interact, EY practitioners can share and learn from an interest in the HLE and parent perspectives. Rather than making judgements or assumptions about the HLE, it is essential to value what parents know and do by making it easy to share communication knowledge about what works between the home and the setting.

The following case study provides an example of the importance of bilateral information sharing between home and setting.

CASE STUDY 6.1 SARAH

Sarah aged three has just started at her local preschool setting. She has delayed spoken communication, and staff and children find it very hard to understand her although she has a good understanding of much of what is spoken to her. Sarah is very interested in 'doing' things' and gets involved in physical activities within the nursery, particularly in the outdoor area. However, she seems uncomfortable at group and carpet times and has become rather withdrawn in her relationships with other children.

In discussing Sarah's communication with her parents, they indicate that, at home, they use Makaton signs and symbols with Sarah who is used to using signs as a way of making herself understood more clearly. They have also set up a strategy where they use a wide range of Makaton symbols throughout the home environment which Sarah can access to make her needs known, make choices, start conversations and repair miscommunications.

They comment on the signage around the setting and the fact that some areas of the setting and some resources have been symbolised, but that neither staff nor children appear to refer to these and that the symbols are not overtly supported by any signing or wider communication strategies. They note that this seems to have confused Sarah and resulted in some level of avoidance of verbal interaction.

REFLECTION 6.1

- *After reflecting on the case study above involving Sarah, consider the following points: As a practitioner, are you interested, engaged and receptive to children and their family communication methods?*
- *What could you do to enhance your practice in this area? Be mindful of how you can develop consistent information-sharing between your setting and the home learning environment.*

Positive relationships

Research into children's SLC development focuses not only on the quality of the EY setting but also the HLE. In its longitudinal study of children's learning and development, the Effective Provision of Preschool Education (EPPE) project (Sylva, 2010) identified the HLE as being the key environment for children's SLC development. As many children now enter EY settings at a younger age, the role of the EY setting becomes increasingly important in offering rich language experiences for children. Sylva (ibid) identified the characteristics of effective practice and the pedagogical approaches which support children's day-to-day learning experiences. In addition, the relationship with the home and family becomes increasingly central to practice. Seeking to understand what works in the home and how communication is mediated is a central part of the practitioner's role as part of the bidirectional relationship. Sharing aspects of good practice with families can be daunting, but the positive relationship with the child has to encompass the family too, and therefore, engaging parents becomes key to the Early Years Practitioner (EYP) role (Bain et al., 2015). The EYFS (DfE, 2024) stresses partnerships with parents. The need for open communication within the mesosystem to break down barriers for parents and build relationships with the home is a challenge to practitioners in supporting parents to recognise the central importance of their parental role.

Approaching parents about their child's SLC can be difficult, which is why positive relationships need to begin at the start. EY practitioners should set the scene for shared communication from the point that the child starts at the setting, introducing a daily information sharing mechanism which is bidirectional. Bain et al. (2015) discuss the need for non-judgemental spaces where genuine information sharing can occur. It is essential to bear in mind that parenting is emotional and complex within the societal systems which surround family life. Parents may be under stress from social media which may promote control-based parent–child communication relationships and EY practitioners are in a strong position to model relational and nurturing current perspectives on communication based in attunement and consistent, sensitive responsiveness in our communicative interactions with children (Grimmer, 2021).

Establishing positive relationships with families is central to the bidirectional perspective within the mesosystem where shared communication is established in order to support the child's learning and development. This should be where parents share their expertise and knowledge of the child. Taking the perspective of the Te Whāriki curriculum in New Zealand (Ministry of Education, 2017), the child asks five questions of their setting and its staff:

> *Do you hear me?*
>
> *Do you know me?*
>
> *Can I trust you?*
>
> *Do you let me fly?*
>
> *Is this place fair for us?*
>
> (Vesty and Wardle in Woods 2014)

These questions can equally be applied to parents, as practitioners envisage how they could respond to these questions, thus giving parents a voice in their child's early education and acknowledging the value of listening to parent's perspectives. While it is undoubtedly important for settings to ask parents, 'what can we do for you?' it could be argued that it is even more critical to ask, 'what can we learn from you?'

REFLECTION 6.2

- *Reflect on ways that you can show a deep interest in the parent's perspective and ask what they find that helps their child to communicate.*
- *Recognise what your setting can learn from families about their child's preferences and communication style.*
- *Consider how you share positive evidence about what the child is doing and remember those things that a parent may value.*
- *How do you raise possible concerns with parents? Bear in mind the importance of maintaining ongoing communication.*
- *Be mindful of your own expertise in the key-person role in building relationships in discussions with family and others in the child's world.*

Enabling environments

In the home, emotionally responsive parent–child relationships provide underpinning for optimal development. Awareness of child's emotional responses through a warm and sensitive carer response provides the optimal environment for listening, understanding and communicating. It follows then that, in a setting, the baby room, where practitioners communicate understanding and acceptance, is where good practice in SLC starts (Havighurst et al., 2019). EY practitioners who spend lengthy periods with children in their key-person role in the baby room will need to tune in to all of a baby's non-verbal cues, vocalisations, gestures, facial expressions and behaviours. Working with parents in creating the earliest communication experiences for babies in the setting is especially crucial. If practitioners seek to understand from families about aspects of their child's preferences, interest and routines, then they are more likely to be able to maintain naturalistic and relevant conversations which will also include reflection and recognition of a baby's home language in the provision and environment.

When considering planning an enabling environment in the setting for supporting SLC, the phrase 'a language-rich' environment is often used but not always clearly articulated with specific practice examples. However, it is important to be mindful that this is not just about resources or room arrangements. Practitioners should reflect on the elements that can constitute 'language-rich'. Primarily, children will talk more when they have something to talk about and someone who is really listening and, therefore, the practitioner themselves will be an essential element of the environment. Hayes and Rooney's 2019 research has a focus on the quality of children's everyday experiences in EY environments. This research suggests that adults who are attuned to children, not just to the provision of resources, have a positive impact on children's early learning and communication experiences. This attunement is best supported by a genuine interest in the child's home and family life.

Learning and development

From a systems perspective, the setting is where many elements of the child's microsystem interact, where there is a crossover between health, education, community and family. The concept of interagency working is often worked out within the educational setting which becomes the place where parents, practitioners and other professionals may work together or share information (Skinner et al., 2019). EY practitioners can contribute significantly to the shared discourse in the interagency arena as they share their knowledge of the child, gathered through daily observations and planning, to build up a holistic perspective over time of the child's communication skills. However, once a child begins to attend a setting and, if other professionals become involved, parents may feel deskilled and less secure in their own role as the child's main communication partner. Hence, the focus of a number of early intervention programmes has been on helping parents to develop their confidence in supporting their child's early SLC. EY practitioners have a central role to play, not just in guiding the child's learning and development but also in getting to know parents and supporting them as partners in their child's learning and development.

Real-world examples

In the second half of this chapter, findings from a small-scale research study are presented to reflect the voices of a parent and a practitioner in an example of good practice in working with children's SLC. This project was a pilot study for the writer's PhD research into understanding the shared working practices in supporting children's SLC. Interviews with a parent and a practitioner within a local EY setting were analysed, and key themes relating to working together were identified.

Theme one – relationship

When asked about the ways in which staff and parents worked together, trust was a significant element of the findings about the relationship between staff and parents. This practitioner explains the care that she takes when sharing information about a child's SLC with parents to support and build a trusting relationship:

> *We don't want to find feel like we're putting additional pressure on parents or make them feel like they're doing something wrong, like "Hey, this is what you should be doing." Some parents would see it as that whereas some parents would be really grateful for the information. It's all about knowing, not necessarily just the child, but the family as a whole. And with the parent, knowing how they're going to take it, knowing what information they're going to want...... because we don't also want to be seen as a judge in their parenting. We seem to be quite good at reassuring parents and parents seem to accept what we say especially as we know their child. There's a trust relationship there. I do think that's something that's really important in any kind of aspects of learning and development that you have to trust the people that are caring for your children.*

From the very first interaction with a family, the foundations of building trust commence. A strong and effective relationship between staff and parents is paramount, and it's vital that interactions in the infancy of the relationship are carefully managed. Parents need to feel that they can leave their child knowing that they are going to be cared for and kept safe.

Be mindful that parents may not have spent any time away from their child when approaching a nursery for childcare. In that case, the settling in process for both the child and the parent is important, particularly if there are any SLCN. As a part of the process, parents should be given dedicated time to feel that they are able to share all about their child so that they are valued and heard. Practitioners need to be mindful of the emotional state of the parents and offer reassurance that their child will be ok.

REFLECTION 6.3

Think of a child you know who attends an ECEC setting.

- *Has the child ever been separated from their parents before?*
- *What are the family dynamics and relationships?*
- *Are there any early concerns about the child's SLC?*

Now reflect on how your awareness of these aspects might influence the way in which you communicate with the child and the parents.

Focus on some specific things which you might do to make the child and family feel part of the setting.

When settings allocate key children for practitioners, often parents will gravitate towards a practitioner. Often the first practitioner that greets the parent or has the initial communication can be who the parent instantly makes a connection with.

This parent, who has a child with some early concerns about their SLC, discussed the strong relationship with the setting staff, and here, we see the value of the key person knowledge born out of time spent with the child:

> *Preschool definitely helped so much, and they obviously spend a lot of time with her . . . . . .they know her like really well. She's not been over there that long because she just moved up from the nursery to the preschool. But even when she was at the nursery they would come and visit and get to know her still. So yeah, ... I think once they spend so much time with the child, they get to know her and they sort of understand her a lot more.*

Theme two – communication

The research project being discussed identified aspects of knowledge about communication and the way in which this is shared. Both parent and practitioner discussed the whole-setting communication strategies which are clearly personalised and included:

- Daily handover routines.
- Bidirectional online platform to post observations, videos and share 'wow' moments.
- Care diaries.
- Open access to conversations with staff.
- Listening to parent concerns.

The parent clearly valued the online system in particular:

> *I can also upload things about what she's been doing at the weekend and if she's .... done anything amazing I can put that on there, photos as well and then obviously when I drop off in the morning I also say, "oh this weekend she's been to the zoo so she's quite tired today" and just letting them know what she's been up to or how she's feeling that day.*

Online messaging platforms enable parents to send direct communication of in-depth information that they wish to pass onto staff members at any time (or late hour). However, this does have some disadvantages being bidirectional, as written dialogue can be misinterpreted. Likewise, if there is the option to message, this can limit parents wanting to speak to staff members directly. This can have an effect on the relationship between parents and staff, and there is no substitute for face-to-face verbal communication. So, although there are now multiple strategies to communicate with parents, the most important are the verbal handovers on arrival and departures. The handover is key for families to share everything about the child on arrival, including personal care information, but also what life for the family has been like. A large part of the daily handover can be that parents get a few uninterrupted minutes to offload and share how they are. This rapport with parents supports the open communication that is needed between the practitioners and parents, especially when there needs to be referrals or additional support sought for the children.

The practitioner spoke about how she valued parent's direct questions at drop-off and pick-up:

> *It kind of opens a gateway then for you to say, well, actually he's not necessarily saying as many words as I'd expect. But I said as long as we keep talking, you tell me your concerns. I'll make sure that I keep you up to date with what I'm doing. I explain the whole process.*

Theme three – access to support

Parental permission is vital for settings to seek additional support for the families. For some families, when a practitioner suggests that there may be reasons for your child to be given additional support, they can feel overwhelmed or disagree that this is the case. Thinking that there is something wrong or different about your child can be isolating and difficult to process. This can often be the reason that families decline any help and support, and communication between the setting and the family can break down.

An honest relationship from the staff is vital, as parents need to be completely on board with the ideas and give consent for information to be shared.

The practitioner in this research study recognises the sensitive nature of these issues:

> *Obviously, nobody likes to be told that maybe your child needs a little bit of extra support ...but also the earlier the better. I think for parents as well, sometimes it can be a bit of a shock when all of a sudden, you're telling them (their child) is maybe not developing way you'd expect them to when in it's never been mentioned to them before.*

This parent with concerns about their child's SLC suggests that the system takes time to negotiate and expresses how the nursery is working with her to help her to negotiate the system:

> *They're all trying to sort of support that (referral process) at the moment so nursery are helping to get her on track for that. The nursery will do a report which I then take with me to the 2yr check. .... and I guess it will all come together eventually but at the moment it's quite separate we're just trying to hit as many routes as we can to sort of get the help we need as quickly as we can 'cos I know these things take quite a lot of time.*

In the interview, this parent also makes a strong case for other agencies to take note of the knowledge, skills and insights of the EY practitioners whom she clearly trusts and appreciates their level of knowledge about her child:

> *And any outside agency, they'll get a really short time with her, so they won't know the full picture. I know it sounds horrible, but they need to see her on her worse days. That's when she needs most support.*

REFLECTION 6.4

Considering the case studies and perspectives presented within this chapter, what can you do in your practice to make interagency communication and additional support mechanisms work for your children and families?

CHAPTER SUMMARY

This chapter has explored some of the essential elements of pedagogy and practice in working with the whole family to support children's SLC. In particular, it has presented a challenge to practitioners to give space and time to getting to know parents, show respect for parental insights and value parents as credible knowers when operating in this sensitive area of children's development.

In engaging with insights from professional reflecting on their own practice, they have emphasised the importance of a consistent whole-setting approach to working alongside parents while recognising the need for each child and family to be seen as unique.

The views of parents have also been used to support a fuller recognition of the things which parents value in this area.

KEY QUESTIONS

After engaging with the content of this chapter, consider the following:

- *How do you plan to develop a whole-setting approach to SLC so that parents can feel confident in the knowledge and skills of the whole setting team?*
- *We often talk about parents as the child's first educators. Consider how this works in reality for your own children and families.*

Further reading and resources

https://speechandlanguage.org.uk/
Speech and Language UK have a range of material for educators as well as resources which you can signpost parents to.

https://www.froebel.org.uk/
The Froebel Trust has useful resources; just go to their website and put 'parents' into a search.

7 JOINING THE GENERATIONS

LAURA SANDERS

THIS CHAPTER

By actively reading this chapter and engaging with the material, you will be able to:

- Explore examples of professional practice and links to theory to support the rationale and reasoning for the importance of intergenerational play sessions.
- Reflect on how intergenerational play can contribute to children's microsystems (Bronfenbrenner, 2004) and communication and language (C&L) development.
- Use practice examples to encourage you to seek your own experiences of intergenerational play to support the development of supporting children's communications in your future practice.

Introduction

The aim of this chapter is to provide a research case study to inspire and contextualise how children's speech, language and communication (SLC) can be promoted through intergenerational play. This chapter is different from other chapters in this book as it provides a detailed account of how children's SLC has been encountered and promoted in a context that may be unfamiliar to you as a practitioner. The tone of this chapter is driven by the story, emotions and experiences of the author.

I have been very privileged to share this research journey with my son Harvey who attended the intergenerational play sessions when he was 2-4 years old from 2016 to 2019. Harvey has given his consent to be included in this chapter and has excitedly shared his thoughts five years on from when he last visited the centre. I have also been mindful of what Harvey would think about this research in future years (Harcourt and Keen, 2001) to inform what is included. Holt (1991) suggests that close observation of young children by the people who are deeply interested in their development is advantageous. Within this psychoanalytic tradition, I as the observer will reflect on the emotions evoked while watching my son. Harvey's key person within the setting (Whalley, 1997) was also able to observe and share her thoughts about his interactions honestly and openly with myself as a parent and peer. This research has allowed the partnership of home learning and learning through the setting to work collaboratively and support connection between both (Arnold, 1997) which is important, especially when focusing on areas of development such as SLC as discussed in Chapter 1.

The fascination of watching children interact with the elderly is one I will take with me throughout the rest of my career in Early Years (EY) and Education. Harvey's eyes still light up with awe and excitement when we look back at photographs and videos of our time together with the residents. He asks me now, as a nine-year-old, very in-depth questions while reflecting on his own memories. He can recall the residents' names, the activities he did, but most importantly the conversations he would have with the residents. The advantage of working with the elderly residents (although this is suggestive) is that conversations were often repeated weekly, which for language acquisition is key! This is often due to residents forgetting they have spoken about the subject and repeating it – or it has such a large significance that they would always tell the story, again, linking to perhaps forgetting it had been told.

Harvey will often ask to go back to see the residents; however, as time has moved forward, many of the residents sadly are no longer at the centre. Donaldson (1987) discusses how real-life experiences and opportunities place significance to effective learning. I can report that Harvey's time spent at the centre has provided significant benefits to his holistic development, but in particular his C&L. This will be explored throughout this chapter.

Where did the idea begin?

In 2016, during an OFSTED inspection in my own EY setting, the inspector asked what the nursery offered that nowhere else does. We talked in depth about facilities and places to visit in the local area, but this was the catalyst to where the idea began.

Traditionally, schools would go to care homes to sing to residents at Christmas time, but why did it need to be a stand-alone event? Surely, care home residents need interactions all year round and not just at Christmas. In Elfer's (1996) research, he questions if there is a place for more family-like effective pedagogic strategies in settings. Supporting this, Brennan (2005) labels a 'culture of tenderness' when practitioners help children feel at home with love, patience, humour and attention within the setting. I felt that this could be achieved within intergenerational play sessions and would contribute to promoting children's learning and development.

Following this, I contacted care homes locally and found, only a 10-minute walk away from my nursery, an assisted living centre. This centre has a large communal dining room which is an ideal space to hold play sessions. Residents live in the centre when they require support and care for four hours per day; typically, this is for personal care, meals and socialisation. Each resident has their own flat within the centre but joins in the communal area for social activities and mealtimes.

The beginning of my research needed to explore my own key values and beliefs in relation to working with the elderly. The first time I visited the centre, I felt nervous. I was very apprehensive about the smell – would it stereotypically smell like I expected a care home would smell? There is often a lavender soapy smell, that for some reason I had a convinced myself would be an issue. Of course, it wasn't, and actually, it smelt nice and incredibly clean!

After considering my own beliefs and values, I then sought validation that this was an idea worth pursuing. I explored historical theories to apply my own rationale and reasoning, to which I have over the past eight years been collecting and reflecting upon. The section that follows will highlight the key theoretical perspectives that have underpinned the approach taken in this research study.

Application of theory

For many practitioners, the Statutory Framework for the EY Foundation Stage (DfE, 2024) and non-statutory guidance become fundamental to delivering EY Education, and there can often be fear to deviate or try something different. Dreikurs (1970) described this as the courage needed to be imperfect. This phrase is key when reflecting on experiences with children and the elderly. Often, the aims of the session can be very different from the outcomes, and for the children, this can often be the most wonderful learning and experiences, especially when considering the value for children's C&L. There is little preparation for the spontaneity of the language used in the sessions, and often, the conversations between the elderly and the children are the catalyst for the rest of the time at the centre. Nimmo and Hallett (2008) discusses that there is separation from real life where children are segregated from society, with the electronic age influencing many children learning about history through television and internet, rather than speaking to those that may have experienced it. Nimmo and Hallett (2008) states that if children are participating directly in a community, this is also likely to create meaning to the community.

This links to the proposals from Malaguzzi (1993, p. 72) that children are 'autonomously capable of gaining control of the adult world'. Malaguzzi (1993) views children as being competent and active learners, who are capable of participating in real life. Bronfenbrenner et al. (1984) suggest that research has indicated that the presence of children in the home affects the quality and quantity of a family's social network, supporting that there is a positive outcome likely from the interactions between the residents of the centre and the children.

Thinking about the impacts on community, the visit from the children to the centre has become for many residents, the highlight of the week. The visit from the children often encourages the residents to be up, dressed and ready in the communal area for the children's arrival. I often would arrive early with Harvey, and we would greet the residents as they entered the communal space. Harvey would assume the role of leader and direct the residents where to sit and would, even at two years old, help them to move their wheelchairs and walking frames to the side, out of the way. A particular highlight for Harvey was a resident's mobility sooter. He would repeatedly ask the resident what each button did with his favourite phrase 'what that do?' and the resident would repeatedly share what every button did. His particular favourite was the button that went beep!

The non-verbal interactions were the most fascinating. Some residents had limited verbal communication due to illness such as a stroke but would make eye contact with the children. Their excitement over throwing balls onto a parachute and offering people items as if they had never seen them before was infectious. Residents that had limited mobility suddenly were able to throw a ball onto a parachute because a child had given them a ball. The children would give instructions, either verbally or non-verbally, for the resident either through speech or gesture to throw it (and they would with little hesitation). The inclusivity of the play sessions always seemed effortless. Children and residents interacted non-verbally through the sharing of resources. Smiles and eye contact were the encouragement children needed to engage. The children's interactions with the residents, which, for many children, are outside their day-to-day experiences, support a child's cultural capital (Bourdieu, 2000).

You might think of a child's cultural capital as children carrying around a bucket with them. Each day, new language, experiences, risks taken and places visited contribute to learning. When this learning is significant, this remains in the child's bucket to contribute to their cultural capital. When working with a child in an EY setting, it is important to understand what is in their bucket! The understanding of a child's prior learning and experiences is vital when planning for their SLC development and their overall holistic development. As a practitioner, to understand the value that play and learning gives to a child enables practitioners to effectively enhance and adapt activities to meet the individual needs of children.

Experiences such as intergenerational play visits aim to give children experiences and language for their bucket. So how do we know or measure a child's cultural capital?

All about the child

As shown in Figure 1.1, when considering Bronfenbrenner's ecological model of human development, a child is at the centre with the family, along with EY settings forming key elements of the child's micro-system. Family is the principal context within which human development takes place (Bronfenbrenner, 2004) and when there is a strong collaboration between both this raises outcomes for children. I considered the potential outcomes of the interactions between the children and elderly, which led me to consider if children would have experienced interactions outside of the setting.

When I reflected upon Harvey's first-hand experiences and interactions, I was able to consider his extended family, which is part of Harvey's Mesosystem

(Bronfenbrenner, 2004). Harvey had a Great Gran and Great Grandma still alive before we started the visits to the centre. Both of the great grandparents lived a few hours away from our home, and both were 85 years upwards. Harvey sees his grandparents weekly. They were within the 55-60 age range in 2016. They are able to support with weekly childcare, and I would not consider their interactions to be the same as with the elderly great grandparents. Harvey would excitedly visit his Great Gran's house and would always instantly gravitate to her chair that had the buttons (to help her get out if it or recline), and there was a wooden duck toy that she had always stored out of sight, that even months after playing with it – he could recall it would be there.

When visiting Great Grandmas house, he would repeatedly use the phrase at two years of 'don't touch' as the crystal ornaments lie perfectly placed on the fireplace. The most influential part of the visits was the language. Both Great Gran and Great Grandma would talk to Harvey on our visits continuously. One particular theoretical approach indicates that the ability to develop language is innate (Gopnik et al., 1999; Pinker, 1994); however, McDonagh and McDonagh (1999; pp. 4–5) state that the existence of 'motherese' speech that is produced by an adult (or older child) in interaction with a child whose linguistic competences and cognitive development are perceived as limited. Trevarthen (2002) labels the concept of motherese as a rich musical quality that comes into the voice. Motherese has a special rhythm and melody that could be heard in the Great Grandparents. They would sing traditional nursery rhymes, engage in turn taking language games such as pat a cake and peek a boo. Their communication with children was always with ease, and the response was listened to and heard. There were no distractions such as the television on in the background or mobile phones in hand; the children had direct eye contact and pure focus and time spent on communicating.

Hansen and Hawkes' (2009) research found that being looked after by grandparents has a positive effect on a child's naming vocabulary. Naming vocabulary is just as it sounds – naming the day-to-day experiences with the child. One of the potential explanations for this finding is that grandparents may often be providing one-to-one care with the child, thus, more time to talk and share the world with their grandchild. This aligns with my own view of Harvey's experiences with his great grandparents, where time appears unhurried and there are limited technological distractions such as mobile phones. Gray (2005) estimates in the United Kingdom (UK) that around 30% of families with children under five receive some childcare support from grandparents.

This shed light on the need to consider the following:

- What would the children in our nursery's experiences with the elderly be?
- Do they have any first-hand experiences of interacting with the elderly?
- And what about the children's parents? Do they have any first-hand experiences with the elderly?

REFLECTION 7.1

Consider the points above and begin to think about your views on working in an intergenerational way.

- *What are your experiences with the elderly?*
- *Did/do you have interactions with anyone over 80 years?*
- *Are your experiences positive or negative? Why?*

The importance of family

When considering the social context of a family, Allen (2007) captures the notion that as society changes, so too does the family. The historical discourses and perceptions of family must now adapt to the more diverse society in which we live. Allen (2007) highlights that professionals need to have a more sophisticated understanding of family life and understand the differences and changes from the perceived ideal of a nuclear family. For many of the children attending nursery, grandparents are involved in their weekly care and are fit and able. The layers that define Bronfenbrenner's (2004) theory are sometimes likened to Russian dolls, where smaller dolls are placed within much bigger ones (Lindon, 2005). The closest and immediate layer, the child's microsystem, includes the child's interactions with friends and family, which includes grandparents. Having a clear understanding of the child's microsystem supports an effective introduction into the intergenerational play visits which form part of a child's mesosystem.

Bruce (1997) highlights that a child's family and sociocultural background are deeply influential to a child's education and can cause barriers between parents and EY settings. It was important to consider if the values and experiences of the parents would cause any barriers or even lead to refusal for children to participate. It is likely that these experiences will influence their attitude to accessing the EY education for their children, and this will have a profound influence on their child's outcomes (Sylva et al., 2004). Starting the sessions required parents to understand the intended benefits and outcomes of the intergenerational sessions. Parents want their child to be cared for, and an inclusive culture and ethos for the setting is paramount. It is the role of practitioners to ensure accessibility and understanding and to build equal and respectful partnerships with parents. Many parents now also feel that because they are spending less time with their children, potentially due to pressures from the exosystem (e.g. parents workplace), that there is a greater importance on what they do with them (Buckingham, 2000). This would correlate with the interest and eagerness from families wanting their child to participate in the sessions.

Noddings (1984) argues that caring is a universal human concept – because everyone has been cared for and wishes to be cared for – and should be the foundation for ethical decision-making. Maintaining a relevant and responsive approach is vital so that families will engage and want to use the EY services (Whalley, 2006) as well as sharing information with parents to enable them to feel included in the setting and the education of their child. The careful approach and fully informing the families of the intended outcomes and benefits saw 100% of families giving consent of the children to attend the intergenerational play sessions from 2016. For many families, there was an expression that they had not had experiences with the elderly due to there not being relatives for the children to engage with at home. The response from parents was very supportive.

The aims of the sessions

Between the nursery and the centre staff, the main aims of the intergenerational sessions were created, being:

- To provide a physical, active, **language rich** and stimulating adult-led intergenerational play session for children.
- To invite residents to participate and **engage in conversations** and play with children.

Dewey (1933) saw social relationships as crucial to learning, which links to Vygotsky's (1978) view of the Zone of Proximal Development (ZPD), which is the role of the supportive adult. With children, we apply the ZPD when looking at what a child can do on their own, then consider what can be achieved with the support of an adult. The ethos of the play sessions was to engage in an adult-directed activity, and then, looking at what the child can then do with the residents with support. The first activity was always to sing a 'hello' song accompanied with British Sign Language (BSL) signs of names and welcoming everyone to sit in a circle. By starting with saying and singing 'hello' to everyone, names of the residents in the centre were vocalised, and children were able to repeat a song they are familiar with in the setting. Learning names is key to initiating conversation and the feeling of belonging.

Trevarthen (2002) who writes about learning in companionship discusses the desire to know more is within human nature. When considering how we collaborate with others, Huxham and Vangen (2006) discuss the term collaborative advantage. This is considering the notion that it is possible within work to feel inspired. It creates opportunities for learning and addressing moral issues. Having a culture that promotes others to express autonomy and relatedness can also motivate others. People who experience these emotions are more likely to develop a powerful sense of purpose in life (Kotter, 2013). This relates to the role of the practitioners within the sessions. Often, the practitioners would adopt observer roles within the play sessions due to the high levels of engagement and involvement from the children (Laevers, 1997). The staff would position themselves around the circle to support the children to engage with the residents, and to be accessible as a secure base for the children to go to if they are unsure or need comfort during the session.

The importance of interactions

Interactions with children are profoundly important for supporting and extending children's learning and development. When considering the effectiveness of the intergenerational play session on children's SLC, research has attempted to identify and give a definition of effectiveness within conversation. Bruner (1980) reported that only 2% of conversations observed within a research study had connected discourse, a to-and-fro dialogue. In intergenerational conversations, we see the child talk to the resident and then the resident responds. To fulfil connected discourse, the child then needs to reply to the resident's response. The simplicity of the conversations saw Harvey many times have this length of dialogue with residents. Often, the resident would mishear or misinterpret what was said, and then, Harvey would seek out a staff member to help to convey his intended conversations. There are high levels of engagement and high levels of motivation from Harvey to be heard and understood by the residents. He shows determination and persistence to be heard and is a great example of Vygotsky's (1978) notion of the ZPD.

Tizard and Hughes (1984) looked at the differences between interactions children have with adults in their homes and at interactions with adults within schools. They named this notion as the passages of intellectual search which found that questioning by the mother was more effectively supporting children's learning and development than teachers in schools. Children ask many questions while engaging with the intergenerational sessions and by using the adults whom they have an attachment to seek answers to their questions. Children show high levels of engagement (Laevers, 1997) while participating in the sessions, which encourages children to ask questions and seek 'why' things happen. Harvey would ask 'why' questions continuously, and not just with myself as his parent, he would ask his key person. Harvey used his language to help build strong relationships with adults and as he turned three and four years old, with his peers. During many of the sessions, in circle time scenarios, questions would be posed to the group. Harvey had a strong sense of agency and had confident language skills. He would be able to say how he felt and put forward ideas. Using language as a tool for learning (Mercer and Hodgkinson, 2008), the sessions would allow Harvey to describe, explain and often reason and argue. He would often use his strong sense of self to speak up for what he wanted to do and what activities he would want to do next. Often, practitioners can see this sense of agency of being comfortable behaviour, when actually, is an important part of the SLC development.

Working together

When researching how to effectively support children's SLC, there are comprehensive studies, projects and journals all relating to what is effective, or not effective – yet looking at the effectiveness in intergenerational relationships is a new concept, and one that I hope will be documented and shared more in the coming years. The basis of this project is the firm understanding that interactions help to build warm relationships with children, practitioners and the residents in the centre, which is key to developing self-esteem and the confidence to be a successful learner (Roberts, 2002). Field's (2010) views support that the earliest years of a child's life are critical if their potential is to be realised in adult life, while Arendt (1958) suggests that one of the highest realisations of the human condition is to exercise agency (Bandura, 1986). The intergenerational visits allow children to be active agents in their learning. They are given opportunities to show autonomy and exercise their agency (Bandura, 1986). The visits are led by the child in terms of the language and conversations, which leads to higher level thinking, known as metacognition (thinking about thinking). The children are experiencing, and then revisiting experiences, while extending and questioning what happens and why. They are engaging in sustained shared thinking (Siraj-Blatchford et al., 2002) with the residents as every activity or conversation is learning together.

Siraj-Blatchford et al. (2002) introduced the term 'sustained shared thinking' after carrying out a project looking at the relationships and working together to learn. Vygotsky (1978) discusses the 'more knowledgeable other' (MKO) which within sustained shared thinking could be two children or an adult and a child. Children or adults could be the MKO, as both parties contribute to the thinking. This can be described as learning hand in hand and involves investigating and learning together. It is lovely when a staff member is asked a question, is unsure of the answer, and 'hand in hand' (metaphorically) the practitioner and child find the answer together and create a learning moment – worthy of being in their buckets (as mentioned earlier). This can be seen in action in activities at the centre, such as a paper aeroplane activity. The step-by-step process to create a paper aeroplane was demonstrated to the group of children and residents. The process was repeated twice so all children and residents had time to observe and process the instructions. The children and residents were then paired and given paper. The residents seemed to look for the children to take control of the activity, but then children would have difficulty in folding, to which this prompts them to ask for help from the residents. The residents seemed to have a fear of doing it wrong, but they were supportive for the children to try. Bernstein et al. (2008, p. 194) define learning as 'the modification through experience of pre-existing behaviours and understanding', yet often, the elderly residents cannot recall their previous experiences, and as it is the child's first experience, they need support to be willing to have a go. Vygotsky (1978) suggested that children learn the best when they are tackling problems that are just beyond their current level of understanding, but it is vital that the MKO is available to support and guide the learning. The same can be said about enhancing SLC. Having a go at pronouncing and using new vocabulary is necessary if children are to develop within this area.

REFLECTION 7.2

Take a moment now to think about how you feel when learning a new skill.

- *Do you feel the fear of doing it wrong?*
- *Can you think of a time that you have overcome that fear?*

Recalling a moment that you have had the support of a MKO will help you to connect with the stories.

- *How could you apply this learning to speech and language development?*

CHAPTER SUMMARY

Intergenerational practice brings an awareness of others and their needs; the children learn compassion, develop emotional intelligence and a range of social skills necessary to develop relationships throughout their life. Harvey's intergenerational sessions have supported his language and development. At nine years, he can recall his time at the centre, and he reflects and questions his experiences, expanding his speech and language skills in doing so. There is no need to analyse any data to show the sparkle that enters his eyes when we talk about his time at the centre. How much keener are you to share your experiences when you have enjoyed something immensely? Harvey reflects articulately and very accurately, which demonstrates his metacognitive processing and level of quality learning experiences – they are still in his bucket!

Through 'joining the generations', it has on many occasions shown that the elderly are left feeling valued as a resource to young children. Residents can engage in simple activities that can challenge their physical and mental ability, while promoting children's holistic development, in particular their C&L.

This chapter has explored the main concepts of what intergenerational play is and how it can benefit speech and language development. As you continue to read through the chapters within this book, think about the theory and practice examples and reflect on what you have read in this chapter. As awareness and practice examples such as Harvey's are shared – awareness and promotion of the importance of intergenerational experiences will increase. My intention from this chapter was to offer motivation to seek your own experiences for your future practice and, ultimately, have intergenerational play within your cultural capital buckets too.

KEY QUESTIONS

After engaging with the content of this chapter, consider the following:

- *How can you relate Harvey's joining the generations' journey to your own practice?*
- *Do you know about the involvement of children's grandparents?*
- *How well do you understand children's individual cultural capital?*

Further reading and resources

Del Boca, D., Piazzalunga, D. and **Pronzato, C.** (2018). The role of grandparenting in early childcare and child outcomes. *Review of Economics of the Household*, 16, pp.477–512.

Del Boca, Piazzalunga, and Pronzato discuss the impact of early childcare provided by grandparents on cognitive development.

Lane, E.T., Jones, R., Little, R. and **Owen, H.M.** (2020). Intergenerational play. In *Playwork Practice at the Margins* (pp.89–106). Routledge.

The authors of this chapter describe the vision and development of a park designed to inspire intergenerational play.

Sykes, G. (2018). Intergenerational communities: The young and the old together. In *Young Children and Their Communities* (pp.70–84). Routledge.

This book highlights the importance of communities and the rich opportunities they offer to children. The chapter Intergenerational communities focuses on the benefits of intergenerational interaction.

8 COMMUNITIES WITH CHILDREN WITH EAL: MOVING BEYOND THE GUIDANCE IN THE EYFS

SUE HOBSON

THIS CHAPTER

By actively reading this chapter and engaging with the material, you will be able to:

- Explore the stages of second language acquisition.
- Consider the good practice laid out in Early Years Frameworks in the United Kingdom.
- Begin to view bilingualism through a wider international lens.
- Consider the inextricable link between language and culture and how to acknowledge and promote this within an Early Childhood setting.
- Consider how to develop strong links with families when there is no common language.
- Consider how this understanding translates into the Early Childhood learning environment and supports all children.

Introduction

Child:	*'Miss, what language do you speak at home?'*
Practitioner:	*'I speak English'*
Child:	*'No Miss, I mean what language do you speak when you are at your home?'*

For this primary school aged child from Leicester, a city in England with a diverse range of backgrounds, cultures and languages, it was inconceivable that the adult teaching her was unable to speak a second language. Her experience and that of her friends was that everyone was bilingual if not multilingual, that school operated in English, and home and family operated in another language entirely. The chapter that follows will explore therefore what the curriculum offers and how this can be enhanced by an understanding of the inextricable links between language, culture, community and family and what that affords children's long-term outcomes for themselves and society.

Setting the scene

Census data gathered from England, Wales, Northern Ireland (2022) and Scotland (2011) show that over 600 languages are spoken in the United Kingdom (Talbot, 2024).

The European Council Resolution on multilingualism asserts that languages unite people, render other countries and their cultures accessible and strengthen intercultural understanding (2008). However, this positive outlook is not always obvious in educational settings within the United Kingdom where a lack of English may be primarily viewed as a barrier to be overcome as quickly as possible and with the impact on the setting or school data giving cause for concern.

Education Scotland in its Curriculum for Excellence (2017) promotes more than this pragmatic approach. The learning for success in life extends beyond school to the future of the community and the country as a whole and is a clear thread throughout the curriculum. It sees early disadvantage as an indicator for poor personal and national outcomes. Their document Learning in 2(+) Languages (2020) sits within this framework and offers practitioners a practical and theoretical approach to learners with English as an Additional Language (EAL), acknowledging what they bring in terms of key strengths and 'intercultural competencies' understanding that 'this integration in turn helps to create a more cohesive community and society' (2020, p. 4).

Ireland has produced a comprehensive toolkit for EAL support for welcoming primary children who have no English or Irish (Together Towards Inclusion. Toolkit for Diversity in the Primary School, 2007).

The practicality of the toolkit helps educators to consider steps to take in meeting the learning needs of EAL children.

REFLECTION 8.1

It is not unusual for EAL to be considered a barrier to learning.

- *What reasons could there be for this?*
- *In what ways could this belief hinder teaching EAL?*

What do we already know about how an additional language is learnt?

> *A child's first language provides the roots to learn additional languages, and parents should be encouraged to continue to use their home languages to strengthen and support their children's language proficiency as they join new environments.*
>
> (Early Years Alliance, 2022, p. 44)

Too often the emphasis on learning an additional language has focused on how to teach it but Krashen (1982) argues that this does little to understand how children acquire a second language preferring an understanding of process rather than product. The Early Years Foundation Stage Statutory Framework (EYFS) states that 'the development of children's spoken language underpins all seven areas of learning and development' (DFE, 2024, p. 9). It is easy for practitioners to feel pressured to ensure that children with EAL become competent English speakers as quickly as possible. However, an appreciation of the value of the child's first language and the role it plays in their understanding, learning and identity, along with knowledge about the stages of learning an additional language enables a practitioner to plan effectively for the learning of all children.

The Early Years Alliance EAL toolkit (2022) explains how Sequential Acquisition is observed when a first language is established, and a second language is introduced. This usually happens after the child is three. This is the case for many of the children with EAL who may already be early speakers of more than one language, but their exposure to English is new.

Practitioners working with young children with EAL will recognise these different stages of language acquisition:

1 The Silent Period – a child may be silent whilst they absorb what they hear and see and make sense of the world around them.

2 Language mixing – seen in simultaneous acquisition (where two languages are heard from birth) languages are used together in different settings until the child become competent in the use of the language most appropriate to the audience.

3 Code switching – the use of both languages in the same utterance. This may occur when one language is preferred in specific contexts or is used with certain people or to exclude someone in a conversation (Pacey, 2024).

4 Interference – this may occur when a child uses some second language in a first language context.

5 Loss of first language – a child with limited access to their first language and submerged in the second intensively begin to lose access to their first language before they have developed age-appropriate competence in their second.

6 Grammatical errors – as children begin to use a second language, they make errors, confusing tenses, sentence structure, plurals, prefixes, etc.

The silent period can last for up to six months causing concern for those practitioners who do not recognise it as a normal stage of multilingual development. During this time, a child is observing others and absorbing language. Whilst not all children go through this period it is essential to ensure that the silent child is able to access learning appropriate to their cognitive abilities. Bligh and Drury note that 'Children (regardless of their mother tongue) are taught through the medium of spoken and written English in and through all subject areas' (2015, p. 259) and whilst there is an increasing number of bilingual practitioners the majority are still monolingual. Building a relationship with parents and, where possible, collaborating with bilingual colleagues affords an understanding of the child and helps to ensure they have access to an appropriately challenging curriculum.

It is vital that pressure is not put on children to speak in the silent period but practitioners need to be sensitive to opportunities to support a child's readiness to communicate, however this may present, as demonstrated in the following case study.

CASE STUDY 8.1 NOOR

Noor (3y9m) had been in nursery for four months and had not spoken at all. At a pre-start home visit his mother had described him to the bilingual practitioner as chatty, and during regular conversations with her since she reported how he told her about nursery and sang the songs at home. At nursery he appeared shy but played near others whilst observing them. He was slow to join games even though many of the children shared his first language. One practitioner, understanding how communication is more than spoken language, took Noor's eye contact and body language to be communicative and chose to whisper to him, taking his faintly voiced outbreath to be 'conversation'. She persisted and over the course of the next few weeks, Noor began to whisper back using single words then short sentences, and then talk quietly. By the end of the year, he was chatty and confident with an ever-expanding vocabulary.

REFLECTION 8.2

> Non-verbal communication can be particularly useful in sustaining conversations with children.
>
> (Gripton, 2019, p. 78)

Thinking about the case study above and how Noor communicated without words, consider how non-verbal communication can be part of conversation.

- *How could the practitioner in the case study have extended the conversation further?*

The role of play

Play is central to children's learning (Early Education, 2021) and has a key role for a child with EAL. Access to culturally relevant play materials is necessary to support understanding, although children can manipulate their environment to be relevant. For example, the Chinese boy who took the drumsticks into the home corner to use as chopsticks or the five-year-old refugee who packed a suitcase with a sponge and water bottle so that 'I can get money for my family by washing cars wherever we go'. Play allows the exploration and expression of feelings, personal experiences, social interaction, the immediate environment and the world beyond. The sensitive and observant practitioner can support a child's play supplying narratives with appropriate language in context. The freedom of play allows a relaxed environment in which to explore and try out language.

The outside space is equally important and allows a physical freedom where a child can find their voice. One boy, the only Cantonese speaker in the setting, had been silent in the classroom since starting. Once outside he took the role of 'monster' and chased other children whilst roaring and gesticulating. This became a favourite game with a group of children, with whom he later felt able to build relationships and try out his new language.

REFLECTION 8.3

The EYFS Statutory Framework states 'When assessing communication, language, and literacy skills, practitioners must assess children's skills in English' (DfE, 2024, p. 16).

- *How can a child's progress in these areas be assessed during the silent period?*
- *How can this be recorded?*
- *Why does this matter?*

Language and community

Whilst good practice toolkits can support EAL learners in school, their use may limit engagement with embedding community and cultural values as a vital part of education (Sood and Mistry, 2011). Thus, the school community is left with fewer resources to draw on.

The following Case Study describes a Junior school in the East Midlands city of Leicester, England, which is as diverse as the community it sits within. The children bring experience of their own family, faith, culture and the language and knowledge of the community to their learning every day.

CASE STUDY 8.2 SHAFTSBURY JUNIOR SCHOOL: THE SCHOOL

Shaftesbury Junior School lies close to the heart of Leicester City and a stone's throw from Narborough Road. In 2015, this road was the subject of an academic project called 'Super Diverse Streets' finding it to be the most diverse street in the United Kingdom. It remains an area with a fluid population and a diverse cultural community.

The school caters for just under 250 children and has had up to 47 different languages spoken at one time. Children join the school at different stages of their education and not necessarily at the start of the year. They may be new arrivals to the country or have been to several schools prior to coming to Leicester. They can move on from Shaftesbury at any point in the academic year and their place is quickly taken by children on the waiting list of this oversubscribed school.

The impact on school results and the data collected is evident and brings with it local authority pressure to show improvement. The head teacher speaks of realising how a whole school approach to meeting the needs of the children and a creative approach to overhauling processes and practices within the school was vital. Over time a detailed child and family centred proactive induction process was developed ensuring a supportive welcome for each child with named staff and buddies to meet them, and literature and a dictionary in their first language in the room to welcome them.

Assessment and teaching are rigorous and staff aspirations are high, drawing on support from The Northern Association of Support Services for Equality and Achievement (NASSEA) and Local Authority Support ensuring that individual progress is demonstrated. Three mornings a week there is a language class at 8 a.m. Here pre-teaching, vocabulary conferencing and support are offered to an ever-growing group of over 30 children.

Information technology is used to support pupils' learning and is a helpful bridge when children arrive with a language not commonly spoken in school.

Oral and written language is supported by Widget, a visual support system, which is invaluable as a prompt for both comprehension and expression.

The development of staff understanding and skills and the appointment of EAL Lead Staff have budgetary implications but the commitment to all the children is evident. The most recent OFSTED report reports that pupils understand diversity and equality.

The school welcomes opportunities to share good practice with others where possible and links have been made with St Philips Centre. In addition, the school has School of Sanctuary status through the City of Sanctuary organisation resulting in a sound understanding of the fragile situations of those who are asylum seekers and refugees. More information on both organisations can be found in the further reading and resources section at the end of this chapter.

REFLECTION 8.4

After reading the case study above, consider the ways that this school draws on the communities the children represent to support their learning.

- *In what ways could an Early Childhood setting emulate this when the children are at a different developmental stage?*

The St Philips Centre's stated purpose is a commitment to 'working with communities to promote encounter, harbour trust, strengthen understanding and encourage co-operation'. Consider how these purposes are reflected in the commitment of the head teacher and staff to engage with families and help all pupils to be effective learners.

- *In an Early Childhood setting how such a commitment might be realised?*

CASE STUDY 8.3 SHAFTSBURY JUNIOR SCHOOL: THE CHILDREN

On a visit through the classrooms with the head teacher, a straw poll showed that only a handful of children in each class of around 30 children were monolingual.

Of the remaining, more than half spoke two or more languages and many children started school with no English at all.

(Continued)

(Continued)

A small group of pupils at Shaftesbury gave an insight into how children felt when entering a new environment with little or no experience of the school system or English. One boy commented, 'I was very early, and I sat down and then a loud bell went off and people started rushing and I thought "ooh, what's that?"'

They all expressed relief when they heard someone speaking a familiar language but also said that fellow pupils helped them make links with others who spoke the same language as them. The support for each other was evident and the common experience was not that they spoke the same languages but rather that they all spoke a language other than English. This extended to a greater understanding and respect for the cultures of others. When asked what was something that they felt important to say to the interviewer one girl said, 'Don't be rude about (other people's) country'. This respect is fostered in the school through celebration days of other cultures, language of the month and the '30 characteristics of the school' displayed in each classroom and discussed with an emphasis on how these can be demonstrated to others.

They spoke enthusiastically about 'The Language of the Month'. Pupils speaking that language translate for their peers, recount stories and take part in presentations. Two boys were very excited that the next language of the month was Malayalam, their language, and were looking forward to teaching new words to the school and translating for others.

REFLECTION 8.5

These children in the case study above have been encouraged and supported to express themselves. They are respectful of difference and able to celebrate and nurture their own and others' community festivals and important events in diverse and creative ways.

- *What are the key approaches that help this school to be a successful multilingual and multicultural community of learners?*
- *Consider how an Early Childhood setting might engage with the local community to enhance the education of all children and deepen their experience of belonging to a caring multicultural learning community?*

Language, culture and identity

Culture, at its simplest can be defined as 'who you are; the condition of being a certain person' and 'a defining feature of a person's identity', with language 'intrinsic to the expression of culture' (Rovira, 2008, pp. 65, 66). These definitions encapsulate the centrality of language to define who we are, but this is a complex issue requiring a considered response (Siraj-Blatchford and Clarke, 2000). Over time globalisation, conflict and the exercise of power have eroded the distinct cultural identities of peoples by, among other things, the marginalisation of their language. There are moves in many countries to rediscover the expression of cultural identity through a reclaiming of indigenous language.

On 1 June 2008, Canada's Truth and Reconciliation Commission was established to address the continuing impact of residential schools (1831–1996) where generations of First Nation children were removed from their homes and imprisoned in schools where many died and all were forced to reject their culture, language and identity with merciless punishments meted out to those who were reluctant. In 2021, legislation named September 30th as a National Day of Commemoration with the understanding that the attempted annihilation of identity created seismic rifts in generations of people. A First Nations-led initiative, 'Orange Shirt Day' is held at the same time to commemorate this immeasurable loss, reclaim First Nation culture and language and promote the concept 'Every Child Matters'.

Whilst these developments recognise the need for reconciliation, Canada is not new to operating in more than one language. Some states, both in North America and in the United States, have language immersion schools where the languages spoken reflect the culture, identity, political history and government of the area. For example, some French speaking Canadian states have French immersion schools. Children are bilingual from an early age with bilingualism a tangible asset offering greater employment and leadership opportunities and social mobility.

Historically, politics, power and colonialism have resulted in England remaining largely monolingual with English being widely accepted as the lingua franca in many global arenas. In areas of Wales, Scotland and Northern Ireland, an understanding of what has been lost over the years in terms of culture and language, distinct from the United Kingdom's Anglocentric ideology, has led to an expression of cultural identity being realised through a reclaiming of indigenous language in many schools, either as part of the curriculum or as the language of instruction (Matheson and Matheson-Monnet, 2020).

Increasingly diverse populations throughout the United Kingdom require a commitment to understanding the place of language in cultural identity. The EYFS Statutory Framework states that practitioners should 'take reasonable steps to provide opportunities for children to develop and use their home language in play and learning, supporting their language development at home' (DfE, 2024, p. 16). Cultural diversity prompts interrogation of the term 'reasonable steps' alongside the imperative to consider the indivisibility of language, culture and identity. To fail to do so risks limiting the rich fund of learning available to children as demonstrated in the new multidimensional GEAR model of positive outcomes in terms of 'psychological growth, cognitive exploration, linguistic awareness and social re-enforcement' (Chen and Padilla, 2019).

Preparing a rich and engaging environment for learning using culturally and linguistically relevant materials is intrinsic to nurturing the child's first language. Being aware of and challenging assumptions is vital. Gillborn (2008) recognises the danger of stereotyping children through a common definition of a 'black identity' without recognising the diversity of experience across cultures. A one size fits all approach simply will not work.

CASE STUDY 8.4 MISSED OPPORTUNITIES

These two cases demonstrate how not recognising diversity can hinder individuals or whole groups of children.

First:

In one London nursery, staff were concerned that a girl seemed isolated from her peers. It was realised that she was the only Hindi speaker in the class whilst most others spoke Sylheti. Assumptions made about her ethnicity meant opportunities for her to access culturally, and linguistically relevant materials were non-existent.

Second:

A City of Sanctuary playgroup for asylum seeker mothers and children meet weekly with many also attending, or going on to attend, local nurseries throughout the city. The leader expressed regret that she is never contacted by local settings to share information about the children or support regarding asylum issues. This may imply inadequate setting induction processes or a disregard for a more outward looking approach which could form the basis of a deeper understanding of the language, culture and identity of each child and family.

Both of the above case studies demonstrate a disconnectedness between the child's prior life experience and their current experience.

The possibility of such disconnect is minimised in New Zealand where the Te Whāriki curriculum embraces the holistic understanding of the interconnectedness of culture, identity, language and learning and a firm belief in a child's potential. The woven cloth imagery of Te Whāriki 'supports children from all backgrounds to grow up strong in identity, language and culture' (New Zealand Ministry of Education (2017, p. 7). This example of excellence is embedded in the design of both local and national education systems, striving for equity, and viewing the cultural capital of childhood experiences as intrinsic to learning, with new learning woven throughout, strengthened and supported by what already is.

Too often in the United Kingdom a child's lack of English is viewed as deficit, whilst 'failing to recognise and value the skills and experiences they have developed through their home language' (Chalmers and Crisfield, 2021, p. 43). The concept of cultural capital as seen in Te Whāriki lends us insight into the requirements of

Ofsted's Education Inspection Framework (EIF) defining cultural capital as 'the essential knowledge that children need to be educated citizens' (Ofsted EY Inspection Handbook, 2019, p. 31). The concern is not only what settings can add to children's learning but valuing, nurturing and building on early life experiences. The reliable starting point for an understanding of cultural capital is the unique child (Cowley, 2019) and for those children new to English, the language, culture and knowledge they bring with them needs to be reflected in their nursery experience. If that culture goes unacknowledged, then what they bring to their learning is misrepresented and limits the effectiveness of the learning environment.

REFLECTION 8.6

- *How can knowledge of the Te Whāriki curriculum support practitioners' understanding of the EIF cultural capital requirement?*
- *What does this make you think about how you would practice with regards to this?*

Language and family

The Early Years Curricula in each UK country focuses to a greater or lesser degree on how building relationships with parents plays a key role in understanding the unique child. The Scottish early years framework acknowledges how 'an understanding, appreciation and respect for the values and beliefs of migrant families, can be a highly effective means of improving the involvement of migrant parents in their children's and their own education' (Scottish Government, The Early Years Framework Part 2, section 2, 2009).

Evidence shows that good home–school relationships can help develop a setting that values what multicultural learners bring (Chalmers and Crisfield, 2021). Minority language parents, unused to the UK education system, tend to be less engaged and involved with school or supporting school learning. Schools that explicitly value and validate students' home languages can promote a rise in cultural capital for minority and immigrant families and allow them to feel connected and supported (Duarte, 2011).

This is evidenced in The MANDELA Model for Early Childhood Education and Care which has inclusivity at its core and fosters a sense of belonging and respect (Lumsden, 2023). To initiate and nurture this with families, practitioners must look creatively at building positive relationships with parents from all backgrounds.

Small-scale initiatives offer opportunities to support parents understanding and engagement with their children. The course 'Family skills: improving EAL learners' literacy through family involvement' (EEF 2018) covered a range of topics over

11 weeks for parents of 4-5-year olds but found that engagement proved difficult. A previous small-scale project managed to encourage engagement by inviting the parents into a Family Story morning in the nursery followed by a learning session with the practitioner and one parent translating for the group (Hobson, 2001). These approaches need committed leadership with significant financial and staffing implications needing to be sustainable over time. Practitioners need to be aware of the far-reaching impact of not engaging with families whose support is needed for children to maintain their first language. Losing it results in family language barriers, with individuals commenting that they feel excluded from their culture and community (The New Yorker, 2021).

The extent of the impact of the pandemic on children's education is only just being realised. Some practices necessarily changed to accommodate regulations. Children were met at the nursery door where they left their parent. In some cases, this persists because it is argued that children settled quicker. Whilst this may be the case, settings need to weigh up what has been lost in terms of family contact and whether parents can feel truly welcomed when they are excluded from the space. Practitioners need to think creatively how they build a 'broad bridge' into their setting, especially for diverse families, to make it straightforward to truly be partners in their child's learning.

REFLECTION 8.7

- *How can the Early Childhood practitioner create a 'broad bridge' approach to welcoming multilingual, culturally diverse families?*
- *What would you recommend to a setting that was struggling to engage with parents?*

CHAPTER SUMMARY

We do a disservice to all our children if we see teaching English as an additional language as one directional and one dimensional or as the implementation of a set of useful strategies to support the acquisition of English. The depth of sharing, the celebration of all cultures and languages creates a sense of belonging, pride, acceptance and self-worth and fosters a willingness to take risks with language, conversations and relationships for all our children.

This approach goes hand in hand with thoughtful, creative and high-quality teaching.

It provides a wider social and cultural appreciation and understanding that 'we are far more united than things that divide us' (Cox, 2016) and helps secure a lifelong engagement and participation in an ever changing and developing world.

When asked to share the thing he thought was most important for others to hear about learning another language, one young bilingual learner declared emphatically,

'Be brave! Speak out!'

Good advice for us all.

KEY QUESTIONS

Having read this chapter and using the requirements of the curriculum framework as a starting point, consider the following questions.

- *How would you develop a Welcome and Induction policy that embraces the opportunities presented by a multilingual and multicultural Early Childhood setting?*
- *How could you build on this framework to embed family involvement and thereby enhance children's learning?*

Further reading and resources

St Philip's Centre https://www.stphilipscentre.co.uk
The St Philips Centre's stated purpose is a commitment to 'working with communities to promote encounter, harbour trust, strengthen understanding and encourage co-operation'.

City of Sanctuary. https://cityofsanctuary.org
The City of Sanctuary states that they are 'a growing network of more than 1000 primary and secondary schools, nurseries and sixth forms all committed to creating a culture of welcome, understanding and belonging for those forced to flee'.

Smidt, S. (2020). *Creating an Anti-Racist Culture in the Early Years: An Essential Guide for Practitioners* (1st ed.). Routledge. **https://doi.org/10.4324/9780429290022**
In this book, Smidt details examples of anti-racist practice from personal research and theory and discusses how racism can be recognised and challenged in early years settings.

9 EVOLVING MULTIAGENCY APPROACHES IN EARLY CHILDHOOD SPEECH AND LANGUAGE SERVICES

NYREE NICHOLSON

THIS CHAPTER

By actively reading this chapter and engaging with the material, you will be able to:

- Explore the historical developments in early childhood speech and language services and their impact on current practices.
- Consider the role of multiagency approaches in enhancing service delivery and the challenges they face.
- Explore the differences in service provision across various geographical regions and their implications for equity and access.
- Investigate the effectiveness of integrated services like Sure Start Centres in supporting speech and language development.
- Examine the impact of socio-economic factors on the availability and quality of speech and language services.

Introduction

This chapter investigates the evolution of multiagency approaches in early childhood speech and language services, offering a historical and geographical overview. The chapter is pivotal for understanding how historical shifts and regional differences have sculpted the landscape of speech and language therapy (SLT) in early childhood. As readers navigate through this chapter, they will uncover the transformation of SLT from isolated, clinic-based services to comprehensive, community-focused interventions that engage multiple agencies.

The primary aim of this exploration is to highlight the significance of collaborative approaches in enhancing the accessibility and quality of speech and language services. This chapter will examine pivotal developments, such as the transition of service responsibility to the National Health Service and the introduction of Sure Start Centres, and how these have influenced current practices across the United Kingdom. Moreover, it discusses the disparities in service provision across different regions, reflecting on the sociopolitical and economic factors that drive these differences. By understanding these dynamics, professionals and stakeholders can better navigate and influence the evolving landscape of early childhood developmental support.

Historical overview of early childhood and speech and language services

SLT services in the United Kingdom have undergone significant transformations over the decades, influenced by both political changes and advances in understanding effective therapy environments. During the 1970s and 1980s, services were typically clinic-based. However, this approach was reconsidered after research suggested that children learn new skills more effectively in meaningful contexts, i.e. environments familiar and relevant to them (Law et al., 2000). This led to a paradigm shift from the 1990s, with therapists increasingly working directly in schools and homes to minimise the clinical setting's potential to induce anxiety and maximise therapeutic outcomes (Law et al., 1998). The change meant that services were embedded within educational settings, closely aligning with schools to deliver care. This placement within the local authority educational domain shifted when it became the responsibility of the National Health Service (NHS), marking a significant transition in the management and delivery of these services (Law et al., 2000). However, funding cuts have affected the availability and scope of these services, impacting support quality and accessibility for children (Brady, 2019; Longfield, 2019).

Prioritisation within SLT services has become necessary due to resource constraints over the past decade, focusing on children with the most severe needs first, which can delay intervention for others (Hall, 2005; Parveen, 2019). This system of prioritisation, while necessary, highlights challenges in balancing immediate demands against equitable service distribution. In the context of early childhood speech and language services, the prioritisation process involves distinguishing between universal, targeted and specialist levels of support. Universal services include routine health checks, developmental screenings and basic advice for parents and caregivers. For example, health visitors conduct regular check-ups and more specifically at two-years old and assess developmental milestones to ensure children are meeting expected. Targeted services, on the other hand, focus on children identified as at risk of developing speech and language issues or those showing early signs of delay. These services offer additional support through more frequent monitoring, group interventions and specific educational programmes.

Specialist services cater to children with significant speech and language needs that require intensive, individualised intervention. These services typically include individual therapy sessions with speech and language therapists, detailed assessments and tailored intervention plans. Additionally, they involve multidisciplinary teams from health, education and social care sectors. The prioritisation process assesses children to determine the appropriate level of service required, ensuring that those with the most severe needs are prioritised first. This structured approach allows Early Years Practitioners (EYPs) to allocate resources effectively, providing the necessary support tailored to each child's specific needs and the severity of their condition.

Sure Start centres: Central Hubs for integrated care

A pivotal development in SLT services was the introduction of Sure Start Centres by the New Labour government from 1999, aiming to create a one-stop-shop for children and families at the heart of communities. These centres were designed to consolidate child support services under local government oversight to help to alleviate poverty and enhance the quality and accessibility of childcare and related services (Bouchal and Norris, 2014). Sure Start Centres exemplified a multiagency collaborative approach, integrating health, education and care services. Their establishment was part of a broader policy aiming at increasing social mobility from an early age, adopting strategies from the American Head Start model and focusing on areas identified as deprived (Barlow et al., 2007; Belsky et al., 2007).

Sure Start centres played a crucial role in supporting speech and language development through various integrated services available within walking distance for most families, from conception of the child until the start of primary school (DfE, 2013). The collaboration across different sectors within Sure Start Centres has been recognised as one of the most effective examples of multiagency collaboration in the United Kingdom, significantly enhancing service delivery and impact (Robinson and Cottrell, 2005; West et al., 2016).

The evolution of SLT services from an education-based, clinic-oriented approach to a more integrated, community-based framework reflects broader social and political shifts, including an emphasis on public health and preventative services. Early years services are crucial in addressing the developmental needs of children, particularly those with speech, language and communication needs (SLCN). A significant milestone in this journey was the development of SLT working through Sure Start Centres as part of their multiagency remit in cooperation in delivering comprehensive and accessible speech and language services.

An effective model of this integrated approach is Nottinghamshire's Children and Families Partnership Speech and Language Therapy service, operating within Sure Start Children's Centres (McDonald and Young n.d.). This service provides accessible specialist SLT for children up to three years old who are at risk of unmet SLCN needs, preventative early intervention for children identified at age two as being at risk of long-term language difficulties, and universal services to support all children in achieving their communication potential. Their focus on building an evidence base for their public health approach has significantly improved service quality and contributed valuable insights to the field of early years SLT. The Bercow 10 Years On report in 2018 highlighted their innovative efforts, showcasing best practices in integrating research into clinical practice to enhance outcomes for children. Despite challenges related to funding and prioritisation, these initiatives represent a progressive step towards a more inclusive and supportive framework for addressing the SLT needs of children across the United Kingdom.

REFLECTION 9.1

- *Given the prioritisation necessary within SLT services due to limited resources, how has this affected service delivery in your setting?*
- *Consider the impact of prioritising children with the most severe needs first and share any strategies that have been implemented to manage or mitigate delays for others.*

National vs. local multiagency support structures

Throughout England, the provision for children's SLCN varies significantly due to differing terminologies and operational frameworks across regions and agencies. These discrepancies affect the uniformity and effectiveness of support services. For instance, terms like 'late speakers' or 'language delayed' can have different meanings in various studies and contexts, which complicate the identification and treatment processes for SLCN (Paul et al., 1997; Raschle et al., 2015).

At the national level, successive UK governments have recognised the importance of speech and language skills as foundational to educational success and have implemented standardised tests such as the Early Years Foundation Stage (EYFS) Profile, Standardised Assessment Tests (SAT) and General Certificate of Secondary Education (GCSE) that require robust speech and language competencies (Standards Testing Agency, 2015; DfE, 2018). However, despite the establishment of integrated services such as the Sure Start Centres by New Labour, which provided access to speech and language therapists, the provision has often lacked consistency (Anning et al., 2005; Bercow, 2008, 2018). However, new research stresses the significant long-term impact of early interventions on GCSE outcomes. Sure Start has been shown to generate significant improvements in educational performance, particularly for children from low-income backgrounds. Children eligible for free school meals living near a Sure Start centre improved their GCSE performance by three grades compared to similarly disadvantaged peers without Sure Start access. These findings highlight that well-designed and well-funded early childhood interventions can produce significant educational benefits and reduce disparities in attainment, highlighting the need for consistent and robust early support services (Carneiro et al., 2024).

The Bercow Review (2008) highlighted a 'lack of equity' in service provision across the country. This inconsistency was addressed partially by the subsequent Better Communication Research Programme (2010), which yielded extensive data yet failed to elicit sufficient governmental response to unify or adequately fund the necessary services (DfE, 2012). In contrast, local initiatives often reflected more directly the specific needs of their communities but experience unequal resource distribution, leading to what is sometimes referred to as a 'postcode lottery' in service availability (ICAN, 2019). Local authorities and Clinical Commissioning Groups have considerable variations in budget allocations for SLCN, which impacts the level and quality of support available to children (Longfield, 2019). The impact of these variations is profound. For instance, while some localities may benefit from investments in early intervention and identification programmes, others may experience cuts in funding, leading to long waiting times for SLT services and significant disparities in the support available (Bercow, 2018; RCSLT, 2017). Such inconsistencies are not only a matter of budget but also reflect the socio-demographic characteristics of each locality, which influence the prioritisation of resources and the strategic deployment of services.

Before 2020, the discourse around SLCN was fragmented, lacking a unified, operational definition that could be universally applied. This fragmentation presented a significant barrier to the effectiveness of both national policies and local initiatives. Existing literature and governmental reports offered extensive data but few actionable insights to guide a more equitable distribution of services. Additionally, there was a notable gap in understanding how local socio-demographic factors influenced the allocation of resources and services, further complicating efforts to address SLCN effectively. The variation in support across different geographical locations underscored the need for a more cohesive and well-funded strategy. By addressing these gaps, there is now an active attempt to create a more unified and effective approach to supporting children with SLCN across the United Kingdom.

Nevertheless, recent developments suggest a shift towards a more unified discourse. The Royal College of Speech and Language Therapists (RCSLT) (n.d.) has provided a comprehensive definition of SLCN. This definition includes issues with producing speech sounds accurately, stammering, voice problems such as hoarseness and loss of voice and difficulties understanding and using language. Additionally, it encompasses challenges with interacting with others, understanding non-verbal communication and using language for questioning, clarifying or describing. This clarity in definition is crucial for developing a national framework that not only sets out clear standards for SLCN but also supports Speech, Language and Communication (SLC).

In 2020, the government developed guidance to support children's SLC, which includes an Early Language Identification Measure and Intervention Tool for use with children aged two to two and a half (Gov. 2020). This guidance is available for all professionals working with children, including directors of public health, directors of children's services, clinical commissioning groups (CCGs), providers of SLT services, providers of health visiting and school nursing services and early years and school settings. The comprehensive nature of this guidance ensures a cohesive approach to supporting children's SLCN.

Multiagency efforts vs. localised initiatives

The following section explores the findings from a research study that sought to explore the how EYPs in two geographical areas supported children with SLCN (Nicholson, 2020). One location is in northeastern England, and the other is in the east coast of England.

Health visitor involvement

EYPs across both locations expressed mixed experiences with health visitors acting as a referral route to SLT services. Historically, health visitors have been a major referral source, but there have been frustrations due to varying levels of engagement depending on the geographical area (Broomfield and Dodd, 2011). Delays in completing health assessments, such as the integrated two-year review, have been noted as particularly problematic, impacting the timely identification and support of children's needs (Nicholson and Palaiologou, 2016), with some EYPs stating that work was often duplicated within early childhood settings due to health visitor delays.

Referral processes and waiting times

The referral process to SLT services notably differs between regions. In some areas, referrals are not accepted until a child reaches three years of age unless additional needs are identified. This policy has been influenced by economic constraints and a 'watchful waiting' approach, potentially delaying intervention (Everitt et al., 2013). EYPs have highlighted that such delays can extend until a child is nearly ready for school, which may impact their readiness and development. However, Nelson et al. (2006) highlighted that this was a useful strategy to see if the child recovered without intervention.

Multiagency support

Support from SLT services showed considerable variation across different locations. Six of the seven EYPs from one location reported that they had never received direct SLT visits to their settings nor had any direct contact with SLT professionals. In contrast, location two noted a more collaborative approach, with regular therapy sessions and training conducted within the early childhood setting. Moreover, in certain regions, joint training involving the child, their family and the EYP was also reported. This variance indicates that multiagency collaborations are more effective in some areas than in others. The training provided by SLT services to both EYPs and families is designed to ensure consistent support across home and educational environments, thereby enhancing the child's development through a coordinated approach.

In all regions, EYPs noted the use of support sheets provided by SLT services, which they often found to be generic and applied broadly across many different children with differing speech and language needs. This generalisation led to EYP frustration due to the lack of tailored support. In some areas, these sheets are integrated into a collaborative approach, where SLT professionals first modelled strategies and then provided the sheets as support prompts. However, in other regions, the same sheets are distributed with minimal customisation, indicating a trend towards cost-saving measures at the expense of individualised care. Frequently, these sheets were handed directly to parents, who were then responsible for relaying the information from SLT to the EYPs. This method risked important details being lost in translation. Such an approach highlights a broader issue within public health strategies where universal tools are implemented without sufficient customisation, potentially reducing their effectiveness in meeting specific needs. This situation highlights the importance of not only what is implemented but also how it is implemented to ensure the effectiveness of support provided.

The effectiveness of SLT services is influenced by the interplay of multiagency efforts and localised initiatives, with significant variations noted across different geographical regions. While some areas benefit from robust multiagency collaborations offering timely and tailored support, others face challenges due to economic constraints and systemic inefficiencies. Terminological differences further complicate the landscape, affecting the uniformity and effectiveness of the support provided. EYPs continue to navigate these complex systems, employing various strategies to advocate for and meet the needs of children with SLCN. This analysis underscores the need for more standardised practices and enhanced communication between agencies to improve the overall efficacy of support services.

REFLECTION 9.2

- *How can EYPs in your setting effectively collaborate with health visitors, speech and language therapists, and other professionals to support children with SLCN?*

Consider both the challenges and solutions related to varying levels of engagement and support from these collaborations, as well as how EYPs can proactively contribute to shared assessments.

- *How do national policies and local initiatives balance in your practice for the provision of SLCN services?*

Evaluate their impact and propose improvements to enhance the effectiveness of these services in meeting the specific needs of your community.

- *How do socio-demographic factors affect the allocation of resources for SLCN in your area?*

Share observations on how these factors have influenced service provision and suggest changes to promote equitable resource distribution.

Once you have answered the questions above and considered your own viewpoint on this, read the case study below:

CASE STUDY 9.1 DIANE'S EXPERIENCE

As an EYP, I have encountered numerous children with SLCN in our setting. One such case involved a three-year-old boy who was non-verbal. When he began at the setting, his parents informed us of his language delay, yet they had not sought assistance from other professionals. The setting referred him to speech and language therapists, who scheduled a Zoom call with the child and his parents for an assessment, with a potential face-to-face appointment following if required. While waiting for the appointment, our setting decided to assess the child and provided various communication support strategies. Using the Welcome tool, we found his understanding to be age appropriate. We introduced a communication book, and we modelled its use with him. When using the book EYPs witnessed progress with his communication, and he started using words like 'help' and 'thank you'. After attending the Zoom call and a subsequent face-to-face appointment, it was highlighted that the communication book had significantly aided his development. However, both his parents and our setting noticed a lack of support from speech and language therapists. Despite this, with the EYPs assistance, the child now effectively communicates using his book. Follow-up appointments are scheduled to monitor his progress every three months with speech and language therapists.

REFLECTION 9.3

Consider the case study above.

- *How can EYPs effectively advocate for and support children with SLCN when external professional resources are limited or delayed?*

EYP experiences across geographical terrains

In Nicholson's (2020) study, EYPs from two areas discussed service variations. EYPs from location one revealed significant challenges in multiagency collaboration for child development services. Health visitors often failed to respond, complicating efforts to conduct essential developmental checks. Resources were notably scarce, impacting children's timely access to interventions such as SLT. For instance, certain referral criteria delayed support until the child reaches a specific age, despite earlier identified needs. EYPs attempt to bridge gaps by involving various specialists like special educational needs and/or disabilities coordinators (SENDCos) and early years teachers to plan and implement developmental strategies. However, the effectiveness of these measures is limited by the specialists' availability and the absence of specific expertise, particularly in speech and language.

CASE STUDY 9.2 INTER-AGENCY COOPERATION AND RESOURCE ALLOCATION

These accounts from EYPs highlight the pressing need for improved inter-agency cooperation and resource allocation to support early intervention and enhance developmental outcomes for children.

Resourcing

Location 1: *'I've tried the health visitors... they never ring back or say "I don't have that child anymore on my books." Even with a two-year check... it doesn't work in practice'.*

Location 2: *'It's due to severe lack of resources... impacting on children's development. We referred him to speech and language, but they wouldn't look at him until he was three'.*

Support and proactive working

Location 2: *'The early years teacher can be left because they're very busy... then three months down the line, I'm still waiting for somebody to come in and observe the child'.*

Location 2: *'I can get in contact with them at any time... I see them at least once a month. They're always available on email as well'.*

Location 1: *'I got the early years teacher in to observe... and the infant school, and we share the care. I'm in the process of referral to community paediatricians'.*

Location 1: *'Our early years teacher is amazing... she would be there on Wednesday afternoon. It would be a lot better if someone from speech and language came in'.*

Early and integrated interventions with family involvement and strategy sharing

Location 2: *'He went for a two-year check... flagged up by the health visitor... referred him to speech and language, but they wouldn't do anything until he turned three'.*

Location 2: *'It's difficult to isolate speech and language... lots of other issues as well. He's now got an Educational Health Care (EHC) plan with support from speech therapists and educational psychologists'.*

Location 2: *'They (SLT) invited us to do specific training with his grandparents. Sharing strategies and information was quite nice, and it was arranged by speech and language'.*

In the context of collaborative work among various agencies to support children with developmental challenges, EYP's highlighted the critical role of early and integrated interventions. Early identification at health checks can lead to recommendations for specialised support, where further developmental concerns, particularly in speech and language, can be addressed. Speech and language therapists, alongside educational psychologists, play pivotal roles, even before formal assessments and plans, like EHC plans, are fully established. The EYPs' insights highlighted the necessity of a responsive and adaptable support system that involves not only immediate interventions but also ongoing, customised support tailored to each child's needs. They also stress the importance of family involvement and the sharing of strategies among caregivers to bolster collective knowledge and support networks. This proactive and inclusive approach is crucial in facilitating meaningful progress in children's developmental journeys, demonstrating the impact of multidisciplinary collaboration in early childhood education settings. These varied EYPs' experiences highlight the importance of robust, responsive and well-coordinated support systems in early childhood education settings.

In the comparative analysis of early years services in two locations, EYP's insights highlighted a dichotomy in multiagency collaboration effectiveness as detailed in Nicholson's 2020 study. In location one, significant obstacles in inter-agency cooperation were evident, with health visitors appeared to be frequently unresponsive and developmental checks delayed. This disjointed communication was compounded by insufficient resources, particularly affecting SLT, where children's support was deferred due to bureaucratic criteria rather than developmental need. Conversely, location two exhibited a more integrated approach with proactive measures, including early identification and intervention, facilitated by robust speech and language support and continuous educational psychologist involvement. This contrast highlighted location two's effective use of a responsive and inclusive support system, emphasising the critical impact of seamless collaboration and resource availability on early childhood developmental outcomes.

REFLECTION POINT 9.4

- *Considering the disparities in service provision highlighted between the two geographical locations, what strategies could be implemented to ensure more equitable access to essential resources such as SLT?*
- *Reflecting on the case where Early Years Professional (EYPS) had to wait for children to reach a certain age before receiving support, how can early years professionals more effectively identify and address developmental needs earlier, despite systemic constraints?*

Coordinated efforts: enhancing language development in early childhood

The importance of a multiagency and multifaceted approach to supporting children's SLCN is vital, especially in an era of budget constraints and dwindling resources in health and education sectors. Consequently, there is an even more pressing need for more inventive ways of resource sharing to bolster children's language development.

The preceding section illustrated a case where a local health authority implemented specialised training for the child, their parents/carers and the early years setting. This strategy ensured a uniform approach to nurturing language development, aiming to decrease the frequency of visits required by speech and language therapists and, potentially, to reduce the overall budgetary demands on each involved agency.

A pilot study by McKean et al. (2022) found EYPs were uncertain about the exact methods of supporting children through interventions. It was also a concern that while interventions were necessary, they should not postpone the intervention by speech and language therapists. Fisher (2023) highlighted the extensive impact of the COVID-19 pandemic on children's health services, noting that over 73,300 children were awaiting service interventions. The distribution of wait times was as follows: 21% waited between zero to 4 weeks, 44% 4 to 18 weeks, 31% 18 to 52 weeks and 4% more than 52 weeks. These statistics underscore the critical need to maximise collaborative efforts across services.

Despite the clear benefits, the adoption of unified strategies varies across UK local authorities. Hayes (2023) pointed out that different local authorities have adopted diverse methods to support children's language development, engaging a combination of SLT, Public Health Nursing, Children's Centres, and EYPs. This variability highlights the necessity for a coordinated, nationwide approach to effectively support early language development in children. The Nottinghamshire case study

(McDonald & Young, n.d.) illustrates this need, showing how public health SLT services are integrated with Sure Start Children's Centres, but also how the evaluation and sharing of best practices are essential for service improvement. However, the lack of uniformity means that while health resources may be coordinated, EYPs are not always informed and integrated into the process. This further supports the call for a systematic, cohesive strategy across all local authorities to ensure that early language support is both effective and universally accessible.

REFLECTION 9.5

- *How can early years settings advocate for these changes within their local authorities?*
- *Given the limited availability of specialists, particularly in speech and language, and the reliance on non-specialist staff such as early years teachers for immediate support, what strategies can be developed to enhance the skills and knowledge base of non-specialist staff? How might these strategies help bridge the gap in specialist support, providing immediate and effective interventions until more tailored support becomes available?*

Some resources to support non-specialist staff in supporting language development and intervention can be found in the Further Reading section of this chapter.

CHAPTER SUMMARY

This chapter has explored the significant transformations within early childhood speech and language services, focusing on the shift towards multiagency collaboration and its benefits in enhancing service delivery. The historical overview provided illustrates how changes in policy and practice frameworks have shaped the current landscape of SLT across different geographical regions.

A critical insight from this discussion is the crucial role of understanding and addressing the dynamics of multiagency collaborations. These collaborations are essential for providing comprehensive and accessible speech and language services that can effectively support early childhood development. The evolution and impact of initiatives like Sure Start Centres and more recently Family Hubs has the potential for integrated services to create robust support networks for children and families. More information on these initiatives can be found in the further reading and resources section of this chapter.

(Continued)

(Continued)

As we move forward, it remains imperative for professionals and policymakers to continuously evaluate and adapt these multiagency approaches. By doing so, they can ensure that all children, regardless of their socio-economic or geographical background, receive the necessary support to thrive in their speech and language development. Building on the discussion of multiagency collaboration, the next chapter examines a practical example of how EYPs and speech and language therapists can work together to support children's communication and language development. It highlights specific strategies, training opportunities and case studies that demonstrate the benefits of an integrated approach. This exploration provides a roadmap for fostering effective partnerships to ensure all children receive optimal support for their development.

KEY QUESTIONS

After engaging with the content of this chapter, consider the following:

- *How can technology be integrated into multiagency collaborations to enhance the effectiveness of speech and language services in early childhood?*
- *What are the long-term outcomes of early childhood speech and language intervention on educational achievements and social skills in later stages of child development?*
- *In what ways can parent involvement in multiagency settings be improved to ensure consistent support for children's speech and language development at home?*
- *How can services be adapted to better support children with speech and language needs from non-English speaking backgrounds within the United Kingdom?*

Further reading and resources

BBC's Tiny Happy People https://www.bbc.co.uk/tiny-happy-people
BBC Tiny Happy People provide activities to help develop children's communications skill.

Education Endowment Foundation https://educationendowmentfoundation.org.uk/early-years-evidence-store/communication-and-language
Resources to support communication and language development in the early years.

Speech and Language Resources https://speechandlanguage.org.uk/educators-and-professionals/resource-library-for-educators/

Free resources for educators and professionals, designed to help you support the 1.9 million children facing challenges with talking and understanding words.

Sure Start Children's Centres https://www.gov.uk/find-sure-start-childrens-centre

Sure Start centres give help and advice on child and family health, parenting, money, training and employment.

Family Hubs https://familyhubs.campaign.gov.uk/

Family hubs offer support to children, young people and their families. They provide a single place to go for support and information from a variety of services.

10 WORKING IN PARTNERSHIP TO SUPPORT EARLY COMMUNICATION AND LANGUAGE DEVELOPMENT

DAVID MCDONALD, BIBIANA WIGLEY AND JULIA HARRIS

THIS CHAPTER

By actively reading this chapter and engaging with the material, you will be able to:

- Reflect on the importance of early years settings and early years practitioners (EYPs) for children's communication and language (C&L) development.
- Reflect on how optimal C&L development can be supported by a range of people and services working together.
- Understand more about the role of Speech and Language Therapists (SLTs) in supporting all children's early C&L development.
- Understand more about different ways in which EYPs and SLTs can work together and what facilitates this.
- Consider how you might apply this learning in practice to improve outcomes for the children you work with.

Introduction

Communication and language (C&L) abilities – such as taking turns in conversation and expressing thoughts, feelings and ideas – are key life skills, helping children to make friends, manage emotions and learn. Scottish early years practice guidance (Scottish Government, 2020) reminds us that the importance of C&L skills for *all* aspects of children's lives 'cannot be overstated' (p. 24).

One of the most important factors for developing strong C&L skills is early years education. When children attend a high-quality early years setting where routines, learning opportunities and interactions with adults are consistently stimulating, they develop stronger language skills (Melhuish et al., 2015) and go on to better learning outcomes at the end of Key Stage 1 (Department for Education, 2021).

However, many early years settings in the United Kingdom currently find it difficult to support C&L development in the way they aspire to. There are two key reasons for this. Firstly, an increasing number of children need extra C&L support. Ninety percent of early years settings in Northern Ireland have seen a recent increase in the number of children with speech, language and communication needs (SLCNs) (Royal College of Speech and Language Therapists, 2024), and the number of two-year olds in England who do not meet the expected level for C&L development increased by more than 40% between 2019 and 2023 (Office of Health Improvement and Disparities, 2024). The reasons for this increase in need are complex. They include:

- Increased poverty, meaning more children's development is affected by the direct and indirect impacts of not having enough resources to meet their needs. In 2023, the proportion of children in the United Kingdom living in poverty rose to 25%, according to official statistics (Department of Work and Pensions, 2024).
- Reduced funding for child and family services, so less early support is available. For example, local authority funding for children and young people's services was reduced by nearly one-third between 2011 and 2018 (Marmot et al., 2020).
- The impact of the COVID-19 pandemic on some children's early social experiences and access to education and to other services – especially for children who were already experiencing higher levels of disadvantage (Family and Childcare Trust, 2022).

Secondly, many early years settings are experiencing financial difficulties. Many settings find that the rate paid for Government-funded early years education placements does not cover the cost of providing them, a problem that will increase as more children become entitled to Government-funded places in 2024 and beyond (Sylva and Eisenstadt, 2024). Financial difficulties also impact on staff development; lack of money is the most commonly identified reason for practitioners being unable to access continuous professional development (Sakr and Bonetti, 2021). Morale in the sector is low, vacancy rates are high, and over half of nursery staff are considering leaving the sector, often citing their inability to properly support increasing numbers of children with additional developmental needs (Early Education and Childcare Coalition, 2023).

In this difficult context, early years practitioners (EYPs) need more support than ever in their crucial role developing children's language and communication skills. This chapter outlines how EYPs can work closely with Speech and Language Therapists (SLTs) as part of a local system of support, facilitators that can help this to happen and some successful recent examples from around the United Kingdom.

Systems of support

The idea that EYPs are part of a system of support for children's development is well-established in early years theory. Bronfenbrenner's ecological systems theory, explored in Chapter 1, proposes that a child's development is supported by connected systems, including their family, educational setting, local community and wider society. An EYP, then, is a collaborator within a wider system, and the work they do to support each child's C&L development adds to and complements the influence of many others around that child (Bronfenbrenner, 1977).

Curriculum guidance encourages EYPs to apply this in practice. For example, Birth to 5 Matters – guidance developed by the early years sector in the United Kingdom – encourages every early years setting to consider how it supports children both as its own community, and through its relationships with parents, carers and wider communities, including multiagency professional communities (Early Years Coalition, 2021). These professional communities include people who work in health, social care and education services, such as health visitors, local authority early years support services, children's social workers and others. Some local areas also have additional early years services with a specific focus on improving children's early C&L outcomes: Family Hubs in some areas of England (UK Government, 2024), Flying Start programmes in some areas of Wales (Welsh Government, 2024) and Sure Start Centres in parts of Northern Ireland (Department of Education Northern Ireland, 2024).

The role of speech and language therapists

Speech and language therapists (SLTs) are also part of a connected local system. Many EYPs will have worked with a Speech and Language Therapist (SLT) providing assessment, therapy or advice for a child who has SLCNs. Early years curriculum guidance in England, *Development Matters*, highlights this specialist role, advising a referral to an SLT when a child pronounces words incorrectly (Department for Education, 2023a).

However, SLTs can and do have a much broader role to support optimal C&L development for all children within their local system. This involves moving away from a narrow 'expert' model (in which some children – those with SLCNs – are referred for specialist advice and support from an SLT) towards the type of collaborative system outlined above, in which an SLT is one of many people who work closely to support *all* children's C&L development – including children with SLCNs, and those without. This conception of the role of the SLT aligns with the ecological systems theory: the SLT, like the EYP, is part of a connected system.

Just as curriculum guidance encourages EYPs to adopt this way of thinking and working, early years guidance promotes it for SLTs. The Scottish Government's

Ready to Act plan (2016) expects that allied health professionals, such as SLTs, will work with universal services (those which are available for all children without referral) such as early years settings to support all children's development. In England, *Best Start in Speech Language and Communication* outlines in detail how local areas should organise a range of provision and services, including Speech and Language Therapy teams, to work as a collaborative system (Public Health England, 2020).

A practical advantage of working as a system is that it recognises and ensures best use of the skills, knowledge and expertise of everyone in a child's life. SLTs bring several relevant skills and competencies to supporting children's C&L, including expertise in:

- Assessing children's speech, language and communication skills.
- Understanding typical and atypical speech, language and communication development.
- Planning and providing support to develop children's speech, language and communication skills, and helping others do this.

REFLECTION 10.1

SLTs are not the only experts in children's C&L. Consider too the expertise that EYPs have in this area (further explored in Chapter 1 of this book). One of the overarching principles in the Early Years Foundation Stage (EYFS) statutory framework is that 'Children learn and develop well in enabling environments with teaching and support from adults, who respond to their individual interests and needs and help them to build their learning over time' (Department for Education, 2023b, p. 7).

- *Consider the skills and knowledge EYPs use in order to provide enabling environments and teaching and support for C&L.*
- *What are your strengths in this topic, and in which areas would you like to learn more?*

Ways of working together

We can see then that EYPs and SLTs bring different expertise to their local system of support. In this section, we explore different ways in which they can work together.

Training

Every level of initial early years training includes a grounding of knowledge in C&L, from level 2 qualifications through to qualified teacher status. However, many EYPs, once qualified, report a lack of further C&L training. In 2017, most EYPs reported that they did not have good opportunities to access C&L training, even though nearly three-quarters had taken part in little or no in-service training on the topic (Communication Trust, 2017a). Some national attempts have been made to address this gap. Since 2019, the Government-funded Early Years Practitioners Development Programme has been available to some EYPs in England. In 2024, this training and support will be available to EYPs in 152 local areas (Education Development Trust, 2024).

As professionals with C&L topic expertise, SLTs are well-placed to offer training for their EYP colleagues. Indeed, one of the core competencies SLTs are expected to have is the ability to develop the 'knowledge and practice of others' (Royal College of Speech and Language Therapists, 2021; p. 19).

The provision of training for EYPs by their local SLT team can be a first step to these two groups of people working together towards the goal of supporting all children's C&L outcomes; indeed, SLT-delivered training can be an effective way of improving EYPs' confidence and skills and may improve children's C&L outcomes (Clegg et al., 2020).

REFLECTION 10.2

- *What further training would help you develop further knowledge and skills related to children's C&L?*
- *What C&L training opportunities are available to you? Where could you find more opportunities?*

The Communication Trust developed the Speech, Language and Communication Framework (SLCF) for the children's workforce (Communication Trust, 2017b). The SLCF is a tool to evaluate your confidence in speech, language and communication (SLC) across 10 strands (such as typical SLC development or learning English as an additional language), at different levels of detail, depending on your role. You can then use the results to develop an individual development plan.

Training and self-audit tools like the SLCF can help a self-motivated EYP identify areas in which they would like to learn more, and this may lead you to find useful training opportunities. However, when you return to practice after completing training, it can be a daunting task to apply what you have learnt; support from others can help.

CASE STUDY 10.1 SARA'S PROFESSIONAL ENQUIRY

Sara often sees an SLT who visits her setting to support children with SLCNs. She would like to know more about how to identify children with SLCNs and support their C&L in daily activities. The SLT, Alex, tells Sara about training offered by the SLT team. Sara reviews the options and signs up to training courses on:

- ages and stages of SLC development;
- using visual support, including signing;
- strategies to use in daily conversations to develop children's interaction and communication skills.

Following training, Sara identifies that Isaac, one of her key children, is not developing C&L as expected for his age. She tries some of the signs and new strategies. Sara finds using new interaction strategies particularly difficult. She is not always sure if she is doing it 'right'. Over time she notices that Isaac responds to the use of signing but continues to have difficulty using words and sentences.

Coaching

For EYPs like Sara, who has picked up new knowledge and skills and would like to apply them in practice more confidently, coaching can be a useful support. Coaching develops a person's skills and practice through conversation and reflection, often within a sustained professional relationship. It is often used in education to develop practice; a coach supports the educator to reflect on what they know and do on a particular topic or area, and then to decide how to develop their practice based on their individual circumstances (Lofthouse et al., 2022).

Coaching fulfils a recommendation of the Education Endowment Foundations Professional Development Guidance for educators as it 'effectively builds knowledge, motivates staff, develops teaching techniques, and embeds practice' (Education Endowment Foundation, 2021, p. 8).

Coaching is an interpersonal process and needs to be based on a supportive professional relationship. To facilitate this, successful coaches follow a number of key principles including:

- being non-judgemental, encouraging and warm to build rapport;
- recognising and building on existing strengths;
- supporting practitioners to take responsibility for their own development;
- working together with the educator to find ideas and solutions.

Coaches actively listen and use a variety of strategies to provoke support reflection and development. This might include:

- Making observations of practitioner or child behaviour. For example, the coach might say 'you introduced some cars to the activity' or 'Josef looked at you when you said his name'.
- Using tentative suggestion to encourage exploration of practice (for example, 'it seemed that Jana wanted to play for longer').
- Using open ended questions (for example, 'How do you think she would respond if you imitated her in play?').
- Summarising the practitioner's thoughts, observations or reflections to clarify or provoke further thinking (for example, 'you think Miles is more interactive with adults when the environment is quieter').
- Questions that explore practitioners' emotional reactions to strategies they are using or being supported to try (for example, 'how do you feel about letting Bailey choose what to play with and how to play with it?').

If we apply this to C&L practice in the early years, we can see that Sara may find an SLT, as someone whose role involves supporting others to develop their skills in facilitating child development, to be a useful coach.

Notice that a coaching relationship is more collaborative than working together in a training session or programme. Training involves an expert instructor and a learner. However, in a coaching relationship, the coach is not an instructor, but someone who uses topic expertise and coaching skills to facilitate learning and development in the coachee. The SLT-as-coach brings the EYP's attention to their existing and newly learnt skills and knowledge, supports them to reflect on how they use them in practice, and how they might continue and develop their use in the future. As a result, the EYP creates motivation and opportunities for their own expertise and practice to grow.

CASE STUDY 10.2 SARA'S MENTEE JOURNEY

Let's consider how these ideas about coaching might apply to Sara's situation.

When Alex, the SLT who told Sara about the training she recently completed, visits the setting, Sara tells Alex she is finding it hard to use new strategies she has learnt. Alex makes some observations about what she sees and hears as Sara interacts with children that morning. These observations help Sara reflect and to realise that when she tries to use several new strategies at the same time, she finds it hard to remember to use any of them very much. Alex asks Sara what she might do to make it easier to remember. Sara decides to pick just one strategy to focus on – 'commenting'. Over time, Sara notices that she is using the commenting strategy more consistently.

REFLECTION POINT

- *From the coaching strategies described above, consider which Alex used to help Sara reflect and decide what actions to take. What other coaching strategies might Alex have used?*
- *Think about a time when you found it hard to take something you'd learnt and apply it in real life. Which of the coaching principles or strategies outlined above might have helped you?*

Coaching in practice

SLTs and EYPs in Nottinghamshire took part in a coaching approach in the Coaching Early Conversations, Interaction and Language (CECIL) project. Local SLTs worked over a six-month period with private, voluntary and independent early years settings, delivering a C&L training programme and one-to-one coaching sessions for EYPs. The project aims were to help practitioners learn and apply strategies to support C&L development in their everyday interactions, and therefore support optimal C&L development for all children (Dawson et al., 2022).

Using video recordings as the scaffold for coaching conversations, SLTs provided ongoing practice-based support. EYPs made video recordings of their interactions with children they knew and worked with every day, and then reflected on these videos in coaching sessions with an SLT. The videos provided a familiar context that supported practitioners to individualise and apply strategies learnt and explored in the training course. Coaching provided practitioners with time to reflect on their own use of key strategies as well as the impact on children they were working with. As coaching was delivered over time, the SLT and EYP knew each other well, and the SLT understood each practitioner's individual needs and could tailor support accordingly.

The impact of coaching can be seen in Figure 10.1. After training sessions, only 19% of practitioners implemented all 'key strategies' in practice. However, after coaching with an SLT using video recordings to support reflection, learning and then implementation of the key strategies, 94% of practitioners implemented all key strategies in practice. The impact of coaching can also be seen in the response to a later coaching session. Three months later, the proportion of practitioners using all key strategies had dropped to 75%; after a further coaching session, this increased again to 100% of practitioners.

Practitioners reported the key strategies that were focused on during the coaching sessions were the strategies they used the most frequently, were the most useful, and had the greatest impact on children (Dawson et al., 2023).

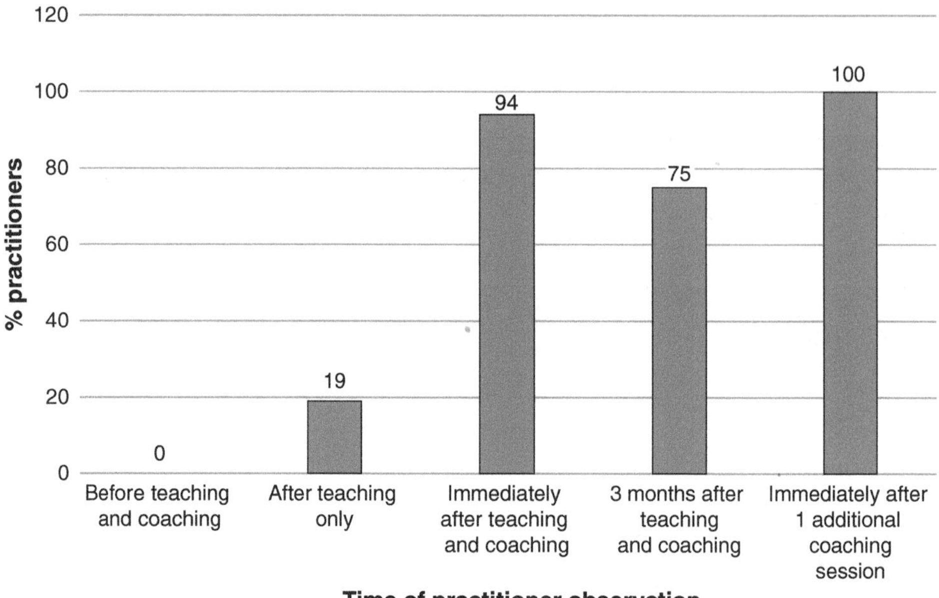

Figure 10.1 Use of key strategies in practice in the CECIL project

Communities of practice

A third way for EYPs and others, including SLTs, to work together is through taking part in a community of practice. A community of practice can be defined as a group of people with a common interest or passion who work together over time to increase their knowledge and expertise (NHS England, 2024).

In relation to C&L, such a group might include EYPs with a particular interest and expertise in C&L developed through training and coaching. The next step – and consider how this is a more system-oriented way to work together – might be to then join a community of like-minded practitioners. Indeed, England's *Best Start in Speech Language and Communication* guidance for local areas identifies the presence of communities of practice as a common feature of local areas which successfully build system working to support children's early C&L development. EYPs within the community of practice might be identified as 'champions' or 'leads' for C&L, and SLTs may have a role facilitating and participating in their local community of practice (Public Health England, 2020).

This opportunity for sustained collaboration is crucial for supporting system working and growing expertise. Kent and McDonald evaluated an early C&L community of practice in Nottinghamshire, England known as the Language Lead Approach, interviewing EYPs who held a 'language lead' role in their setting (Kent and McDonald, 2019). EYPs valued the opportunity work in a sustained, collaborative way with their local SLT to enhance their skills and become the identified C&L expert in their setting. However, it was not only the SLT that brought C&L expertise to the community of practice. EYPs identified too the benefit of the chance to share practice and expertise between EYPs. One EYP explained 'You're in a team meeting, the person who says, "what about language?"... "I know someone in another setting who I've met at a network. I can go and talk to them, and we'll figure it out"' (Kent and McDonald 2019, p. 64).

Facilitators

We have explored some ways that EYPs and SLTs can work productively together to support children's C&L. Many practitioners find, however, that they lack opportunities to do this in practice. The following section describes facilitators which can make this easier or more productive, at the level of systems, settings and people.

Systems

We have explored some of the elements of the complex systems that support children's C&L development. One of the key facilitators to these systems working well is good system leadership in the planning, coordination and delivery of services for children and families. Where good systems exist, services are accessible and sufficient for everyone who needs them, developed together with local people and planned based on a clear understanding of the needs of the areas and communities which they serve (Gascoigne, 2024; Public Health England, 2020).

Leaders in the City of York system in England have taken just such a place-based approach. Senior leaders have worked together to develop and deliver Early Talk for York, a city-wide system to improve C&L outcomes by bringing people together including SLTs, the early years workforce and parents and carers. EYPs access a carefully planned system of training, resources and support which is explained and accessible online in a local 'roadmap' (City of York, 2024). Practitioners report that this system helps them feel more confident in identifying and responding to children's SLCNs, and C&L outcomes in Early Years Foundations Stage (EYFS) Profile results have improved for children in settings which are part of this system (Local Government Association, 2024).

Settings

The influence of leadership is also key at the level of individual early years settings.

As EYPs develop new C&L expertise through some of the professional development opportunities discussed in this chapter, leaders and managers play a key role in supporting them to apply it. As teams develop their C&L practice, setting leaders must develop theirs to maximise the benefits for children. For example, Birro and colleagues explored EYPs' and managers' experience of an SLT-delivered training programme. They found that when leaders participated in and understood training, they were better able to support their practitioners in implementing learning, facilitate peer learning within the setting and develop working relationships with SLTs. Setting leaders identified the importance of their role as 'guides' to help teams apply new learning gained from C&L training (Birro et al., 2024).

People

As well as thinking about the potential positive power of systems and settings, it is important to consider too the social factors that support effective partnerships. In the end, working together is a social endeavour.

Kent and McDonald's study of an early years community of practice in England, described earlier in this chapter, explored a range of barriers and facilitators to success. The importance of individual relationships was clear; SLTs and EYPs alike identified the importance of building professional relationships over time to improve collaboration (Kent and McDonald, 2019, 2021). McKean and colleagues' study of collaboration between SLTs and educators in primary schools in an area of North East England reinforces this point and shows the impact of these relationships on practice; SLTs and educators reported that sustained professional relationships enabled them to understand each other's expertise, feel safe to say when they lacked knowledge or skills and ultimately to exchange skills and ideas to improve C&L practice (McKean et al., 2017).

CHAPTER SUMMARY

This chapter has explored the importance of partnership working to support all children's optimal C&L development in the early years. It has highlighted the importance of the role of EYPs within local systems of support, and a conception of the role of SLTs that is broader and more collaborative than the traditional clinical idea of being a therapist.

For EYPs, this type of partnership working to support children's C&L might involve working with SLTs in training programmes, coaching sessions or a community of practice with like-minded people in order to share and develop local expertise. This is not always easy, and this chapter has highlighted factors that facilitate successful partnership working for C&L. These include influences such as the planning of local services and the quality of leadership within early years settings, and personal factors related to the quality of professional relationships between EYPs and SLT, reminding us that partnerships work well when people have the necessary support, opportunity and time to work together.

KEY QUESTIONS

To help you to apply some ideas from this chapter in your practice, consider the following questions about your role as part of a local system which support children's C&L development.

- *What C&L expertise do you and your colleagues have in your setting? In what ways would you like to expand it?*
- *What C&L training or other structured learning opportunities could you access to help you increase your setting's expertise? What relationships do you have with SLTs or other local professionals, and how could you nurture these or develop new relationships?*
- *What opportunities do you and your colleagues have to develop coaching relationships to support change in practice in your setting? Consider where and how you can be a coach, and where and how you can be a coachee.*
- *How do you link – in an organised way or informally – with practitioners outside your own setting to share and build expertise? How could you do this more, and how would you like it to benefit the children in your care? If there is no existing local community of C&L practice you might join what steps could you take to help develop one?*

Further reading and resources

EEF | Communication and Language (educationendowmentfoundation.org.uk)
These resources demonstrate and explain practices and strategies which support optimal early C&L development. The resources include real-life video examples of practitioners and children.

Home – SLCF – The Communication Trust (slcframework.org.uk)
You can use this framework to assess your speech, language and communication skills and knowledge. We recommend using it together as a whole team in your setting, classroom or room.

HLCP – Higher Level Communication Practitioner | Elklan Training Ltd
This new national scheme for EYPs and teaching assistants can help you support children with SLCNs. One of its aims is to help you link with other people and services to do this. The scheme leads to a Level 4 award for practitioners.

https://www.thebalancedsystem.org/schools/what-is-scheme-for-schools/
This whole system approach can help you plan how you support SLC development in your school or early years setting.

FINAL REFLECTIONS ON PRACTICE AND LOOKING FORWARD FOR NEXT STEPS

The starting point for the book was to examine the leadership role of Early Years Practitioners (EYPs) in this prime area of learning, beginning with the self and interrogating what we bring as students and professional from across practice in the Early Years (EY) to our work with children's SLC. The chapters in this text have provided research-informed perspectives to support pedagogy and practice in the areas of children's speech, language and communication (SLC). Through exploring SLC as a wider issue beyond just a single area of learning and development, the authors have challenged us to reflect on the holistic aspects of children's language development beyond the classroom, with a focus on the contexts of the lives of children, families and communities.

Throughout the text, the authors have represented a range of experiences, knowledge and skills from across the EY sector, from academics and researchers, through allied health professionals to leaders and advisors in EY settings and third sector organisations. The perspectives which they have presented fit across the ecological system as it surrounds and encompasses the child and family. We started the book at the centre of system (see Figure 11.1 below), in the microsystem, considering the child, their family and the environment in which they were situated, and as we moved through the chapters, we have moved steadily towards the outer levels, through the meso, exo and macrosystems to illustrate the impact that various services and contexts can have on young children's communication and language development.

In exploring children's learning and development, there has often been a lack of attention to the social and historical context (Prout, 2005). However, Bronfenbrenner's theoretical perspectives were firmly grounded in his practical concerns around children's early education and care in a sociocultural context (Tudge et al., 2021). However, there are challenges to trying to apply the model to an analysis of practice. Some of those challenges are:

- Complexity of the model.
- Tendency to oversimplify issues or relationships to fit the model.
- An insufficient emphasis on the individual and their own power within the model.
- The child can be viewed as a 'product' of the system rather than an agentic actor within it (Rozsahegyi (in Brown and Ward, 2018, Fleer, 2018; Houston, 2015; Skinner et al., 2019).

Some critiques of the systems perspective suggest that it suggests too much stability, as if frozen in time, and that not enough emphasis is placed on the chronosystem (for example) at the outer region or the biological differences of the individual at the centre (Warren et al 1998). We would also suggest that the neatly drawn systems diagram does not clearly represent the flexibility of boundaries between systems or the permeability of these boundaries as families, professionals and services or provisions move between the different parts of the system or even exist in several parts simultaneously.

Lumsden (2012) argues that the Bronfenbrenner model is likely to be better represented in this way:

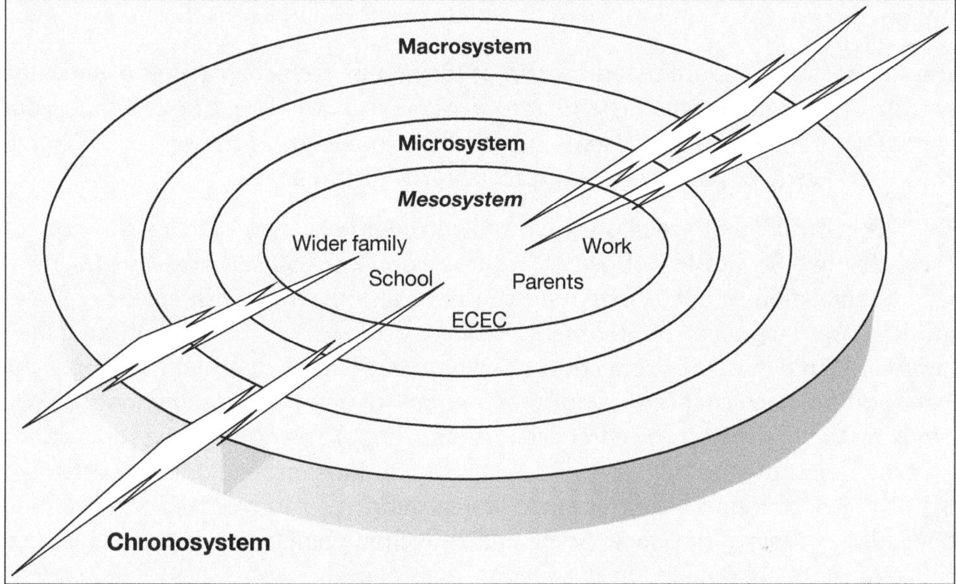

Figure 11.1 Bio-ecological theory with the Chronosystem and Chaoticsystem (Lumsden, 2012)

Lumsden's model (shown in Figure 11.1 above) asserts that the chronosystem exists in order to answer all of the 'why' questions that arise when working with children, and the chaoticsystem is that which blurs the lines between the neatly nested circles of Bronfenbrenner's original model. The chapters throughout this book have shown that professionals from all aspects of health, education and social care work across boundaries, and this can often mean that they are not confined to the neatness that diagrammatic representations of Bronfenbrenner's theory suggest. However, beginning with our relationship with the child at the centre is a useful way to support our thinking and own personal development.

The exploration of the closest aspects of communication practice in the microsystem was supported by Chapters 2, 3 and 4, as the authors gave good practice examples of working effectively to apply communication-enhancing strategies and approaches.

Moving beyond the microsystem, other chapters have also supported an exploration of excellence in practice in working with children's SLC, with evidence from national and international practice and research projects which are operating 'outside the box', for example, in the outdoor and intergenerational learning models outlined in Chapters 5 and 7.

Chapters 6 and 8 considered the impact of the value of communities and families being viewed in partnership with settings. Chapters 9 and 10 built on this with a recognition that support in this area of development is a complex and demanding aspect of practice which involves the need for a strong knowledge about the multiagency context in which EY practitioners work and an awareness of the wider education, health and social care context as it affects children and families in the United Kingdom.

The signposting to additional resources at the end of each chapter has given you a wealth of additional reading and resources with which you can continue your learning journey in this area. Please do continue your learning journey by engaging with these resources and continuing to research in this area.

Key reflection points have allowed you to consider your own practice throughout each chapter. Regardless of which context you find yourself working in, be it health, education or social care, you will have an influence on a child's communication and language development through your work with children and their families. Using these key reflection points should have helped you to apply the learning from each chapter to your practice and for you to consider ways that you can continue to develop your practice further. It should be noted however that this learning does not stop here. We all know that continual professional development is just that – continual – and as such, we challenge you to maintain this learning beyond the covers of this book. Some final reflection points and next steps that you could consider are detailed in the section that follows.

Final reflections on the existing challenges in this area

As you reflect, here are some of the challenges which you may want to consider and think about their implications for children who you work with:

- Current educational imperatives – the emphasis on expectations about school readiness and a narrowing agenda in the EY around literacy as it relates to language development.
- Complexity of community contexts – children's SLC as it relates to poverty and marginalisation is a growing area of concern in policy and provision.
- The implications and impacts of new technology in influencing the changing communication context and the way in which communication relationships are mediated.

Next steps

We hope that the evidence from practice provided in this book will support you to challenge your own practice in the area of children's SLC. The authors have recognised that developing practice and accessing continuing professional development is not easy in the climate of setting budget challenges and funding constraints, smaller local authority support teams and changes to SLT ways of working. However, we would challenge you to be mindful that the characteristics of effective learning (Early Education, 2021) can be applied to us too, so we need to stay curious and be creative.

Developing our practice in SLC is a reciprocal process – it's not just about tracking, assessing and judging children's language output – it's also about children's voices, rights and agency as communicators. As you reflect on the centrality of the enabling communication environment in your setting, consider who is listening to children's voices and how the voices of those with Speech, Language and Communication Needs (SLCN) are enabled. Is the listening, listening with purpose and truly hearing what the children have to say? Children's voices can only make a difference if allowed to by an adult. Policies designed by adults and with parental permission are needed for many things. However, it is argued that children are often allowed to express their views and opinions, but only with adult permission to do so (Gallagher and Gallagher, 2008). As practitioners, in whatever field we find ourselves working, it is important to give children a voice, listen to that voice and then truly hear what that voice is telling us.

REFERENCES

Adams, S E and **Myran, S** (2022) Leader-parent relationships in the early childhood education context: an exploration of testimonial and epistemic justice. *Improving Schools*, 25 (1): 65–82.

Allen, G (2007) Families, in **M Davies** (ed) *The Blackwell compansocial work* (3rd edn.). Oxford: Blackwell.

Anning, A, **Chesworth, E** and **Spurling, L** (2005) *The quality of early learning, play and childcare services in Sure Start local programmes*. Nottingham: National Evaluation of Sure Start Team: DfES Publication.

Arendt, H (1958) *The human condition*. Chicago: Chicago University Press.

Arnold, C (1997) 'Sharing Ideas with parents about how children learn', in **M Whalley** (ed) *Working with parents*. London: Paul Chapman.

Arnott, L (2016) An ecological exploration of young children's digital play: framing children's social experiences with technologies in early childhood. *Early Years*, 36 (3): 271–88.

Arnott, L, **Palaiologou, I** and **Gray, C** (2019) 'An ecological exploration of the internet of toys in early childhood everyday life', in **G Mascheroni** and **D Holloway** (eds) *The internet of toys: practices, affordances and the political economy of children's play* (pp. 135–57). Cham, Switzerland: Palgrave MacMillan.

Bain, J, **James, D** and **Harrison, M** (2015) Supporting communication development in the early years: a practitioner's perspective. *Child Language Teaching and Therapy*, 31 (3): 325–36.

Bandura, A (1986) *Social foundations of thought and action: a social cognitive theory*. Englewood Cliffs, NJ: Prentice Hall.

Barlow, J, **Kirkpatrick, S**, **Wood, D**, **Ball, M** and **Stewart-Brown, S** (2007) *Family and parenting support in sure start local programmes*. Nottingham: DfES Publications.

Barzillai, M, **Thomson, J** and **Mangen, A** (2018). The impact of e-books on language and literacy, In: K. Sheehy and A. Holliman (editors), Education and new technologies: Perils and promises for learners. London: Routledge, pp. 33–47.

Beard, A (2018) Speech, language and communication: a public health issue across the lifecourse. *Paediatrics and Child Health*, 28 (3): 126–31.

Bedford, R, **Pickles, A** and **Lord, C** (2015) Early gross motor skills predict the subsequent development of language in children with autism spectrum disorders. *Physical Therapy*, 91 (7): 1116–29.

Belsky, J, **Melhuish, E C** and **Barnes, J** (2007) *The national evaluation of sure start: does area-based early intervention work?* Brighton: Policy Press.

BERA/TACTYC (2014) *Early years policy advice: Learning, development and curriculum*. British Educational Research Association and Association for the Professional Development of Early Years Educator. London. Available at: http://tactyc.org.uk/wp-content/uploads/2013/11/Early-Years-Summary-Learning-Development-and-Curriculum.pdf

Bercow, J (2008) *The Bercow report: a review of services for children and young people with speech, language and communication needs*. Nottingham: DCSF Publications.

Bercow, J (2018) *Bercow: 10 years on*. UK: ICAN.

Bercow, J (2018) *Bercow: ten years on: an independent review of provision for children and young people with speech, language and communication needs in England*. London: ICan charity RCSLT Available at: www.bercow10yearson.com

Bernstein, D A, Penner, L A, Stewart, A C and **Roy, E J** (2008) *Psychology* (8th edn). Boston, MA: Houghton Mifflin Company.

Beuker, K, Rommelse, N J, Donders, R and **Buitelaar, J K** (2013) Development of early communication skills in the first two years of life. *Infant Behavior and Development*, 36 (1): 71–83.

Billington, C (2016) *How digital technology can support early language and literacy outcomes in early years settings: a review of the literature*. London: National Literacy Trust.

Birro, S, Faulkner, H, Britton, A, Campbell, E, Aghajanian, F, Horesh, A, Lau, V, Munro, N, McCabe, P and **Masso, S** (2024) Early childhood educator and director experiences of speech pathology-led professional development: a qualitative study. *Child Language Teaching and Therapy*, 40 (2): 103–19.

Blackburn, C and **Aubrey, C** (2016) Policy-to-practice context to the delays and difficulties in the acquisition of speech, language and communication in the early years. *International Journal of Early Years Education*, 24 (4): 414–34. https://doi.org/10.1080/09669760.2016.1244046

Bligh, C, and **Drury, R** (2015) Perspectives on the "Silent Period" for emergent bilinguals in England, *Journal of Research in Childhood Education*, 29 (2): 259–74. https//doi.org/10.1080/-02568543.2015.1009589. Accessed 4 April 2024.

Bloom, P and **Markson, L** (1998) Capacities underlying world learning. *Trends in Cognitive Sciences*, 2 (1): 67–73.

Bond, L and **Navarro, D G** (2023) Learning to learn through interaction and motivation. A different view of curriculum and assessment for severe, complex and profound learning disabilities, in **P Imray, L Kossyvaki, M Sissons** (eds) *2023 A Different View of Curriculum and assessment for Severe, Complex and Profoundly learning Disabilities*. London: Routledge.

Bond, S and **Campbell-White, L** (2019) Early years alliance. Available at: https://www.eyalliance.org.uk

Bostock, J R (2020) The application of a flexible learning model to enhance engagement with technologies in language acquisition, *Journal of Perspectives in Applied Academic Practice*, 8 (1): 15–21.

Bouchal, P and **Norris, E** (2014) *Implementing sure start children's centres*. London: Institute for Government. Available at: https://www.instituteforgovernment.org.uk/sites/default/files/publications/Implementing%20Sure%20Start%20Childrens%20Centres%20-%20final_0.pdf

Bourdieu, P (2000) *Pascalian meditations* (R. Nice, Trans.). Cambridge: Polity Press.

Boyatzis, C (1987) The effects of traditional playground equipment on preschool children's dyadic play interaction. In **G Fine** (ed) *Meaningful play, playful meaning*. Champaign: Human Kinetics Publishers.

Brady, D. (2019). 'Lack of funding for children's speech and language therapy' | Public Finance. *Public Finance*. Available at: https://www.publicfinance.co.uk/news/2019/06/lack-funding-childrens-speech-and-language-therapy

Brazelton, T, Tronick, E, Adamson, L, Als, H and **Wise, S** (1975) Early mother-infant reciprocity. *Ciba Foundation Symposium*. 33: 137–54.

Brebner, C, Jovanovic, J, Lawless, A and **Young, J** (2016) Early childhood educators' understanding of early communication: application to their work with young children. *Child Language Teaching and Therapy*, 32 (3): 277–92.

Brennan, M (2005) *'They just want to be with us' young children learning to live the culture: a post-Vygotskian analysis of young children's enculturation into childcare settings*. Wellington: University of Wellington.

Bronfenbrenner, U (1979) *The ecology of human development: experiments by nature and design.* London: Harvard University Press.

Bronfenbrenner, U (2004) *The ecology of human nature: experiments by nature and design.* Cambridge, MA: Harvard University Press.

Bronfenbrenner, U (1977) Toward an experimental ecology of human development. *American Psychologist,* 32(7): 513–31. https://doi.org/10.1037/0003-066X.32.7.513

Bronfenbrenner, U, Moen, P and **Garbarino, J** (1984) Child, family, and community, in **RD Parke** (ed) *Review of child development research,* vol. 7, 283–328. Chicago, IL: University of Chicago Press.

Broomfield, J and **Dodd, B** (2011) Is speech and language therapy effective for children with primary speech and language impairment? Report of a randomized control trial. *International Journal of Language & Communication Disorders,* 46 (6): 628–40.

Brown, Z and **Ward, S** (2018). *Contemporary issues in childhood: a bio-ecological approach.* Oxon: Routledge.

Bruce, T (1997) *Early childhood Education.* London: Paul Chapman.

Bruce, T (2004) *Developing learning in early childhood.* London: Sage publications.

Bruner, J (1980) *Under five in Britain.* London: Grant Mcintyre.

Buckingham, D (2000) *After the death of childhood: growing up in the age of electronic media.* Cambridge: Polity Press.

Cadwell, L (2003) *Bringing learning to life: the Reggio approach to early childhood education.* New York: Teachers College Press.

Carneiro, P, Cattan, S and **Ridpath, N** (2024) *Sure Start greatly improved disadvantaged children's GCSE results.* IFS. Available at http://ifs.org.uk/

Caswell, J and **Peach, K** (2022) When did early years turn beige? *Early Years Educator,* 23 (10): 18–20.

Chalmers, H and **Crisfield, E** (2021) Drawing on linguistic and cultural capital to create positive learning cultures for EAL learners. *Impact,* (5).

Charatan, P. (2006) The target profile diagram. *RCSLT Bulletin,* 647: 20–21.

Chen, X and **Padilla, A M** (2019) Role of bilingualism and biculturalism as assets in positive psychology: conceptual dynamic GEAR model. *Frontiers in Psychology,* 10. https://doi.org/10.3389/fpsyg.2019.02122. Accessed 4 April 2024.

Chomsky, N (1957) *Syntactic structures.* The Hague: Mouton.

Chomsky, N (1976) *On the nature of language. Origins and evolution of language and speech,* 280: 46–57.

Clark, C and **Picton, I** (2019) *Children, young people, and digital reading.* National Literacy Trust. Available at: https://literacytrust.org.uk/research-services/research-reports/children-young-people-and-digital-reading/

Clark, E (1993) *The lexicon in acquisition.* Cambridge: Cambridge University Press.

Clegg, J et al. (2020) Evaluating the Elklan talking matters programme: exploring the impact of a training programme for early years professionals on pre-school children's language development. *Child Language Teaching and Therapy,* 36 (2): 108–25.

Coughlin, A M and **Baird, L** (2013) *Pedagogical leadership.* Ontario: London Bridge Child Care Services & Kawartha Child Care Services.

Coupe-O'Kane, J and **Goldbart, J** (2016) *Communication before speech: development and assessment* (2nd edn). London: Routledge.

Cowley, S (2019) *Defining 'cultural capital' in terms of best practice.* Accessed 23 April 2024.

Cox, J (2016) Available at: https://www.huffingtonpost.co.uk/entry/jo-cox-maiden-speech_uk_5762de5be4b03f24e3db840f. Accessed 20 June 2024.

Cremin, T Hendry, H, Rodriguez, L and **Kucirkova, N** (2022) *Reading teachers: nurturing reading for pleasure*, London: Routledge.

Crowe, K, Cumming, T, McCormack, J, Baker, E, McLeod, S, Wren, Y, Roulstone, S and **Masso, S** (2017) Educators' perspectives on facilitating computer-assisted speech intervention in early childhood settings. *Child Language Teaching and Therapy*, 33 (3): 267–85.

Cunningham, A, Eyre, E, Wood, C, Duncan, M and **Baikousi, V** (2023) *Feasibility study of a Movement and Story-Telling intervention (MAST) for reception children.* Available at: https://www.ntu.ac.uk/__data/assets/pdf_file/0036/2259594/MAST_MainPublicReportFinal.pdf. Accessed 6 June 2024.

Davidson, J I F (2015) Language and play: natural partners, in **D Pronin Fromberg** and **D Bergen** (eds) *Play from birth to twelve* (pp. 175–83). London: Routledge.

Dawson, A, Huxley, C and **Garner, O** (2022) *Coaching Early Conversation Interaction and Language (CECIL) evaluation: implementation and process evaluation.* Available at: https://www.employment-studies.co.uk/system/files/resources/files/Coaching%20Early%20Conversation%20Interaction%20and%20Language%20%28CECIL%29%20Evaluation.pdf. Accessed 9 June 2024.

Department for Education (1990) *The Rumbold report: starting with quality.* London: HMSO.

Department for Education (2012) *Better communication research programme.* Available at: http://www.gov.uk/government/collections/better-communication-research-programme

Department for Education (2013) *Sure Start children's centres statutory guidance. For local authorities, commissioners of local health services and jobcentre Plus.* DfE. Available at: http://childrens_centre_stat_guidance_april-2013.pdf/

Department for Education (2017) *Early Years Foundation Stage Statutory Framework (EYFS).* Available at: https://www.gov.uk/government/publications/early-years-foundation-stage -framework–2. Accessed 2 April 2024.

Department for Education (2018) *Attainment in primary schools in England: quality and methodology information.* England: DfE.

Department for Education (2020a) *Early years apps approved to help families kick start learning at home.* Available at: https://www.gov.uk/government/news/early-years-apps-approved-to-help-families-kick-start-learning-at-home

Department for Education (2020b) *Study of Early Education and Development (SEED): impact study on early education use and child outcomes up to age five years.* UK: HMSO. Available at: https://www.seed.natcen.ac.uk/. Accessed 4 September 2023.

Department for Education (2021a) *Study of Early Education and Development (SEED): impact study on early education use and child outcomes up to age seven years.* Available at: https://assets.publishing.service.gov.uk/media/617a9b79e90e0719751282e4/SEED_Age_7_Impact_Report.pdf. Accessed 9 June 2024.

Department for Education (2021b) *Study of early education and development.* England: DfE.

Department for Education (2023) *Early years foundation stage profile handbook.* England: DfE.

Department for Education (2023a) *Development matters: non-statutory curriculum guidance for the early years foundation stage.* Available at: https://www.gov.uk/government/publications/development-matters–2. Accessed 9 June 2024.

Department for Education (2023b) *Early years foundation stage (EYFS) statutory framework for group and school-based providers.* Available at: https://assets.publishing.service.gov.uk/media/65aa5e42ed27ca001327b2c7/EYFS_statutory_framework_for_group_and_school_based_providers.pdf. Accessed 9 June 2024.

Department for Education (2023c) *Development matters.* Available at: https://assets.publishing.service.gov.uk/media/64e6002a20ae890014f26cbc/DfE_Development_Matters_Report_Sep2023.pdf

Department for Education (2023d) *Statutory framework for the early years foundation stage.*

Department for Education (2024a) Available at: https://help-for-early-years-providers.education.gov.uk/get-help-to-improve-your-practice/working-in-partnership-with-parents-and-carers. Accessed 22 April 2024.

Department for Education (2024b) *Statutory framework for the early years foundation stage.* Available at: https://assets.publishing.service.gov.uk/media/65aa5e42ed27ca001327b2c7/EYFS_statutory_framework_for_group_and_school_based_providers.pdf. Accessed 2 June 2024.

Department for Work and Pensions (2024) *Households below average income: an analysis of the UK income distribution: FYE 1995 to FYE 2023.* Available at: https://www.gov.uk/government/statistics/households-below-average-income-for-financial-years-ending-1995-to-2023/households-below-average-income-an-analysis-of-the-uk-income-distribution-fye-1995-to-fye-2023

Department of Education Northern Ireland. (2024). *Sure Start.* Available at: https://www.education-ni.gov.uk/articles/sure-start. Accessed 9 June 2024.

Dewey, J (1933) *How we think: a restatement of the relation of reflective thinking of the educative process.* New York: D.C. Heath and Company.

Doak, L (2023) Rethinking the contributions of young people with learning disabilities to iPad storymaking: a new model of distributed authorship. *Literacy*, 57(3): 315–26.

Donaldson, M (1987) *Children's Minds.* London: Fontana Press.

Dreikurs, R R (1970). The courage to be imperfect. In **R Dreikurs** (ed) *Articles for supplementary reading for parents.* Chicago, IL: Alder Institute.

Duarte, J (2011) Migrants' educational success through innovation: the case of the Hamburg bilingual schools. *International Review of Education*, 57 (5–6): 631–49.

Dubicka, B, **Martin, J** and **Firth, J** (2019) Editorial: screen time, social media and developing brains: a cause for good or corrupting young minds? *Child and Adolescent Mental Health*, 24 (3): 203–4.

Dunst, C and **Espe-Sherwindt, M** (2016) Family-centered practices in early childhood intervention. *Handbook of Early Childhood Special Education*, (pp. 37–55). Cham: Springer International Publishing.

Early Education (2021) *Birth 2 five matters.* Available at: https://birthto5matters.org.uk/wp-content/uploads/2021/04/Birthto5Matters-download.pdf

Early Education and Childcare Coalition (2023) *Retention and return: delivering the expansion of early years entitlement in England.* Available at: https://www.earlyeducationchildcare.org/early-years-workforce-report. Accessed 9 June 2024.

Early Education (2021) *Birth to 5 matters.* UK: Early Education.

Early Years Alliance (2022) *EAL toolkit.* https://www.eyalliance.org.uk/sites/default/files/somerset_eal_toolkit_17_0.pdf. Accessed September 6, 2024.

Early Years Coalition (2021) *Birth to 5 matters: non-statutory guidance for the early years foundation stage.* Available at: https://birthto5matters.org.uk/wp-content/uploads/2021/04/Birthto5Matters-download.pdf. Accessed 9 June 2024.

Early Years Coalition (2021) *Birth to 5 matters – guidance by the sector, for the sector.* Birth to 5 Matters. Available at: https://birthto5matters.org.uk. Accessed 9 May 2024.

Early Years Inspection Handbook (2019) Available at: https://www.gov.uk/government/publications/early-years-inspection-handbook-eif

Education - St Phillip's Centre (2022) Available at: https://www.stphilliscentre.co.uk/education/. Accessed 30 April 2024.

Education Development Trust (2024) *Early years professional development programme.* Available at: https://www.earlyyearspdp.com/. Accessed 9 June 2024.

Education Endowment Foundation (2021) *Effective professional development guidance report.* Available at: https://educationendowmentfoundation.org.uk/education-evidence/guidance-reports/effective-professional-development. Accessed 9 June 2024.

Education in New Zealand (2017) *Te Whāriki.* Education in New Zealand. Available at: https://www.education.govt.nz/early-childhood/teaching-and-learning/te-whariki/. Accessed 9 May 2024.

Education Scotland (2017) *Curriculum for excellence.* education.gov.scot. Available at: https://education.gov.scot/curriculum-for-excellence/. Accessed 8 May 2024.

EEF. (2018) *Family Skills.* Available at: https://educationendowmentfoundation.org.uk/projects-and-evaluation/projects/family-skills. Accessed 14 May 2024.

EEF (2022) *Assessing the impact of the COVID-19 pandemic on pupil outcomes in Reception.* Available at: https://educationendowmentfoundation.org.uk/projects-and-evaluation/projects/the-impact-of-the-covid-19-pandemic-on-childrens-socioemotional-well-being-and-attainment-during-the-reception-year. Accessed 20 June 2024.

Elfer, P (1996). Building intimacy in relationships with young children in nurseries.*Early Years,* 16 (2): 30–4.

Elsahar, Y, Hu, S, Bouazza-Marouf, K, Kerr, D and **Mansor, A** (2019) Augmentative and alternative communication (AAC) advances: a review of configurations for individuals with a speech disability. *Sensors 22,* 19 (8): 1911-35.

Eng, C M, Tomasic, A S, Thiessen, E D (2020) Contingent responsivity in e-books modelled from quality adult-child interactions: effects on children's learning and attention. *Developmental Psychology,* 56 (2): 285–97.

Ertem, I O, Krishnamurthy, V, Mulaudzi, M C, Sguassero, Y, Balta, H, Gulumser, O, Bilik, B, Srinivasan, R, Johnson, B, Gan, G and **Calvocoressi, L** (2018) Similarities and differences in child development from birth to age 3 years by sex and across four countries: a cross-sectional, observational study. *Lancet Global Health,* 6 (3): 279–91.

Everitt, A, Hannaford, P and **Conti-Ramsden, G** (2013) Markers for persistent specific expressive language delay in 3–4-year-olds. *International Journal of Language & Communication Disorders,* 48(5): 534–53.

Family and Childcare Trust (2022) *Implications of COVID for early childhood education and care in England.* Available at: https://www.familyandchildcaretrust.org/covid-childcare-research-blog. Accessed 9 June 2024.

Ferjan-Ramirez, N, Roseberry Lytle, S, and **Patricia, K. Kuhl, PK** (2020) Parent coaching increases conversational turns and advances infant language development. *PNAS.* 117 (7): 3484–91.

Field, F (2010) *Foundation years: preventing poor children becoming poor adults.* London: Cabinet Office.

Fisher, E (2023) *Growing problems, one year on: the stage of children's health care and the Covid-19 backlog.* Nuffield Trust. Available at: https://www.nuffieldtrust.org.uk/news-item/growing-problems-one-year-on-the-state-of-childrens-health-care-and-the-covid-19-backlog

Fisher, J (2016) *Interacting or interfering? Improving interactions in the early years.* Maidenhead: McGraw Hill, Open University Press.

Flannigan, C and **Dietze, B** (2017) Children, outdoor play and loose parts. *Journal of Childhood Studies*, 42 (4): 53–60. https://doi.org/10.18357/jcs.v42i4.18103

Fleer, M (2018) *Child development in educational settings.* Cambridge University Press: Cambridge.

Fleer, M (2018) Digital animation: new conditions for children's development in play-based setting. *British Journal of Educational Technology*, 49 (5): 943–58.

Flewitt, R, **Messer, D** and **Kucirkova, N** (2015) New directions for early literacy in a digital age: the iPad. *Journal of Early Childhood Literacy*, 15 (3): 289–310.

Floyd, S, **Rossi, G**, **Baranova, J**, **Blythe, J**, **Dingemanse, M**, **Kendrick, K H**, **Zinken, J** and **Enfield, N J** (2018). Universals and cultural diversity in the expression of gratitude. *Royal Society Open Science*, 5 (5): https://doi.org/10.1098/rsos.180391

Forest Schools Education (2023) *Beach schools.* Available at: https://www.forestschools.com/pages/beach-schools. Accessed 6 December 2023.

Franklin, A and **Goff, S**, (2019). Listening and facilitating all forms of communication: disabled children and young people in residential care in England. *Child Care in Practice*, 25 (1): 99–111.

Freeman, K (2022) *Helping children find their voices: a guide for parents and early years practitioners.* London: Routledge.

French, L (2004) Science as the center of a coherent, integrated early childhood curriculum. *Early Childhood Research Quarterly*, 19 (1): 138–49. https//doi.org/10.1016/j.ecresq.2004.01.004

Furenes, M I, **Kucirkova, N** and **Bus, A G** (2021). A comparison of children's reading on paper versus screen: a meta-analysis. *Review of Educational Research*, 91 (4): 483–517.

Gallagher, L and **Gallagher, M** (2008) Methodological immaturity in childhood research? Thinking through 'participatory methods'. *Childhood.* 15 (4): 499–516.

Gascoigne, M (2024) Meeting speech, language and communication needs: a whole-systems, population-based approach. *Paediatrics and Child Health*, 34 (7): 201–10.

Gillborn, D (2008) *Racism and education: coincidence or conspiracy?* Abingdon: Routledge.

Gopnik, A, **Meltzoff, A** and **Kuhl, P** (1999) *How babies think.* London: Weidenfeld and Nicolson.

Grace, J and **Longhorn, F** (2015) *Sensory stories for children and teens with special educational needs: a practical guide.* London: Jessica Kingsley Publishers.

Gray, A (2005). The changing availability of grandparents as carers and its implications for childcare policy in the UK. *Journal of Social Policy*, 34 (4): 557–77.

Grimmer, T (2021) *Developing a loving pedagogy in the early years: how love fits with professional practice.* London: Routledge.

Grimmer, T (2021) *Developing a loving pedagogy in the early years: how love fits with professional practice.* London: Taylor & Francis.

Gripton, C (2019) Communication through the environment. In **J Kent** and **M Moran** (eds) *Communication for the early years a holistic approach.* London and New York: Routledge.

Guernsey, L (2012) *Screen time: how electronic media from baby videos to educational software affects your young child.* New York, NY: Basic Books.

Hackett, A, MacLure, M, and **MacMahon, S** (2021) Reconceptualising early language development: matter, sensation and the more human. *Studies in the Cultural Politics of Education,* 2 (6): 913–29. https://doi.org/10.1080/01596306.2020.1767350

Hall, E (2005) 'Joined-up working' between early years professionals and speech and language therapists: moving beyond 'normal' roles. *Journal of Interprofessional Care,* 19 (1): 11–21.

Hanley, J R (2010) English is a difficult writing system for children to learn: evidence from children learning to read in Wales. In *Interdisciplinary perspectives on learning to read.* pp. 131–43.

Hannon, P, Nutbrown, C and **Morgan, A** (2020) Effects of extending disadvantaged families' teaching of emergent literacy. *Research Papers in Education,* 35 (3): 310–336.

Hansen, C and **Hawkes, D** (2009) Early childcare and child development. *Journal of Social Policy,* 38 (2): 211–39.

Harcourt, D and **Keen, D** (2001) Learner engagement: has the child been lost in translation? *Australian Journal of Early Childhood,* 37 (3): 71–78.

Hart, B and **Risley, T** (1995) *Meaningful differences in the everyday experience of young American children.* Baltimore: Brookes Publishing co.

Havighurst, S, Kehoe, C , Harley, A, Johnson, A, Allen, N and **Thomas, R** (2019) *Tuning in to Toddlers: research protocol and recruitment for evaluation of an emotion socialization program for parents of toddlers.* Available at: https://www.frontiersin.org/articles/10.3389/fpsyg.2019.01054/full

Hayes, D (2023) Supporting communication needs in the early years of childhood. *Children & Young People Now.* Available at: https://www.cypnow.co.uk/best-practice/article/supporting-communication-needs-in-the-early-years-of-childhood

Hayes, N and **Berthelsen, DC** (2020) Longitudinal profiles of shared book reading in early childhood and children's academic achievement in year 3 of school. *School Effectiveness and School Improvement,* 31 (1): 31–49.

Hayes, N and **Rooney, T** (2019) 'I do it all the time! My mam does it!' Leveraging the familiar to enhance communication skills in early years educators, *Early Child Development and Care,* 189 (5): 707–17.

Hinkel, E (2001) Why English passive is difficult to teach (and learn). In *New perspectives on grammar teaching in second language classrooms.* pp. 245–70.

HM Government (2022) *Family Hubs and Start for Life programme guide.* Available at http://family_hubs_and_start_for_life_programme_guide.pdf/

Hobson, S (2001) Culloden nursery family literacy project. In **J. Haggart** (ed) *Walking ten feet tall.* Department for Education and Skills and the National Institute of Adult Continuing Education, pp. 180–2.

Hobson, S and **Farley, C** (2019) Communication and learning dispositions a formula for success, in **J Kent** and **M Moran** (eds) *Communication for the early years a holistic approach.* London and New York: Routledge.

Holmes, H and **Burgess, G** (2022) Digital exclusion and poverty in the UK: how structural inequality shapes experiences of getting online. *Digital Geography and Society,* 3, 1–11.

Holt, J (1991) *Learning all the time.* Ticknall: Lighthouse Books.

Hoskins, K and **Smedley, S** (2019) Protecting and extending Froebelian principles in practice: Exploring the importance of learning through play. *Journal of Early Childhood Research*, 17(2): 73–87.

Houston, S (2015). Towards a critical ecology of child development in social work: aligning the theories of Bronfenbrenner and Bourdieu. *Families, Relationships and Societies*, 6 (1): 53–69.

Hughes, F (2010) *Children, play and development*. London: Sage Publications.

Huxham, C and **Vangen, S** (2006) *Managing to collaborate the theory and practice of collaborative advantage*. London: Routledge.

Iacono, T, **Trembath, D** and **Erickson, S** (2016) The role of augmentative and alternative communication for children with autism: current status and future trends. *Neuropsychiatric Disease and Treatment*, 19 (12): 2349–61.

ICAN (2019) *A Little Less Conversation... A Little More Action Required for Children and Young People with Speech and Language Communication Needs*. Available at: https://ican.org.uk/news/a-little-less-conversation-a-little-more-action-required-for-children-and-young-people-with-slcn/

ICAN (2023) *Speaking up for the covid generation*. Available to: https://speechandlanguage.org.uk/wp-content/uploads/2023/12/speaking-up-for-the-covid-generation-i-can-report.pdf. Accessed 16 April 2024.

Isaacs, B (2012) *Understanding the Montessori approach*. Abingdon: Routledge.

Jarman, E (2013) *Communication friendly spaces*. London: Basic Skills Agency.

Jarman, E (2009) *The communication friendly spaces approach*. Leicester: National Institute of Adult Continuing Education.

Jarvis, S (2013) Capturing the diversity in lexical diversity. *Language and learning*, 63 (1): 87–106.

Johnson, E K and **White, K S** (2020) Developmental sociolinguistics: children's acquisition of language variation. *Wiley Interdisciplinary Reviews: Cognitive Science*, 11(1). https://doi.org/10.1002/wcs.1515

Johnston, K, **Highfield, K** and **Hadley, F** (2018) Supporting young children as digital citizens: the importance of shared understandings of technology to support integration in play-based learning. *British Journal of Educational Technology*, 49 (5): 896–910.

Jovanovic, J, **Brebner, C**, **Lawless, A** and **Young, J** (2016) Childcare educators' understandings of early communication and attachment. *Australasian Journal of Early Childhood*, 41 (4): 95–105.

Kent, J and **McDonald, S** (2021) What are the experiences of speech and language therapists implementing a staff development approach in early years settings to enhance good communication practices? *Child Language Teaching and Therapy*, 37 (1): 85–97.

Kent, J and **McDonald, S** (2019) Collaborative practice in communication for the early years: the learning from a research project, in **J Kent** and **M Moran** (eds) *Communication for the early years: a holistic approach* (pp 57–70). Routledge: Abingdon.

Kent, J and **Moran, M** (2019) *Communication for the early years: a holistic approach*. Oxon: Routledge.

KindredSquared (2024) *School readiness survey: February 2024*. Available at: https://kindredsquared.org.uk/projects/school-readiness-survey/. Accessed 10 April 2024.

Kitzinger, J (1995) Qualitative research: introducing focus groups. *British Medical Journal*, 311 (1): 299–302.

Kokalj, I and **Novak, N** (2023) *Why language development in the natural environment? ELaDiNa Theoretical Handbook*. Available at: https://www.csod.si/uploads/file/PROJEKTI/ELaDiNa/Teoreticni_prirocnik_ELaDiNa_2023_zaSplet.pdf. Accessed 28th December 2023.

Kokalj, I, Kejzar, B, Sack, C, Waite, S, Askerlund, P and **Vollmar, M** (2023) *ELaDiNa practical handbook.* Available at: https://www.csod.si/uploads/file/PROJEKTI/ELaDiNa/Prakticni%20prirocnik_ELaDiNa_ANG_2023_zaSplet.pdf. Accessed 30 December 2023.

Kotter, J (2013) Management is still not leadership. *Harvard Business Review.* Available at: https://hbr.org/2013/01/management-is-still-not-leadership. Accessed 12 March 2021.

Krashen, S (1982) *Principles and practice in second language acquisition.* Oxford: Pergamon Press.

Kusters, A and **Lucas, C** (2022) Emergence and evolutions: introducing sign language sociolinguistics. *Journal of SocioLinguistics*, 26 (1): 84–98.

Laevers, F (1997) *A process-oriented child follow-up system for young children*, Centre for Experiential Education: Leuven University, Belgium.

Landrum, R E, Brakke, K and **McCarthy, M A** (2019) The pedagogical power of storytelling. *Scholarship of Teaching and Learning in Psychology*, 5 (3): 247–53.

Law, J, Charlton, J, Dockrell, J, Gascoigne, M, McKean, C and **Theakston, A** (2017) *Early language development: needs, provision, and intervention for preschool children from socioeconomically disadvantaged backgrounds: A Report for the Education Endowment Foundation.* London: EEF.

Law, J, Boyle, J, Harris, F, Harkness, A and **Nye, C** (1998) Screening for speech and language delay: a systematic review of the literature. *Health Technology Assessment*, 2 (9): 1–184.

Law, J, Lindsay, G, Peacey, N, Gascoigne, M, Soloff, N, Radford, J, Band, S and **Fitzgerald, L** (2000) *Provision for children with speech and language needs in England and Wales: facilitating communication between education and health services.* London: Crown DfEE.

Learning in 2(+) Languages (2020) *Ensuring effective inclusion for the bilingual learner.* Available at: https://education.gov.scot/resources/learning-in-2-plus-languages/. Accessed 14 May 2024.

Lederer, S H (2018) Teaching children with language delays to say or sign more: promises and potential pitfalls. *Young Exceptional Children*, 21 (1): 7–21.

Lindon, J (2005) *Understanding child development: linking theory to practice.* London: Hodder Education.

Liu, S, Reynolds, B L, Thomas, N, and **Soyoof, A** (2024) The use of digital technologies to develop young children's language and literacy skills: a systematic review. *Sage Open*, 14(1). https://doi.org/10.1177/21582440241230850

Local Government Association (2024). *City of York Council: Early Talk for York.* Available at: https://www.local.gov.uk/case-studies/city-york-council-early-talk-york. Accessed 9 June 2024.

Lofthouse, R et al (2022) Understanding coaching efficacy in education through activity systems: privileging the nuances of provision. *International Journal of Mentoring and Coaching in Education*, 11 (2): 153–69.

Longfield, A (2019) *We need to talk report: access to speech and language therapy.* Available at: https://www.childrenscommissioner.gov.uk/wp-content/uploads/2019/06/cco-we-need-to-talk-june-2019.pdf

Lumsden, E (2012) *Early years professional status: a new professional or a missed opportunity.* Doctoral thesis. The University of Northampton.

Lumsden, E (2023) Introducing the MANDELA model – an opportunity for sustainable change? *Nursery World.* Available at: https://www.nurseryworld.co.uk/opinion/article/introducing-the-mandela-model-an-opportunity-for-sustainable-change. Accessed 14 May 2024.

Macmillan, M (1919) *The nursery school.* London: J.M. Dent and Sons.

Malaguzzi, L (1993) History, ideas, and basic philosophy: an interview with Lella Gandini, in **C. Edwards, L. Gandini** and **G. Forman** (eds) *The hundred languages of children: the Reggio Emilia approach to early childhood education* (pp. 41–89). Norwood: Ablex.

Marmot, M et al (2020) *Health equity in England: the marmot review 10 years on.* Available at: https://www.health.org.uk/publications/reports/the-marmot-review-10-years-on. Accessed 9 June 2024.

Marsh, J, Plowman, L, Yamada-Rice, D, Bishop, J C, Lahmar, J, Scott, F, Davenport, A, Davis, S, French, K, Piras, M, Thornhill, S, Robinson, P and **Winter, P** (2015) *Exploring play and creativity in pre-schoolers' use of apps: report for early years practitioners.* Available at: http://www.techandplay.org/reports/TAP_Early_Years_Report.pdf

Matheson, D and **Matheson-Monnet, C** (2020) Indigenous languages of Scotland: poverty culture and the classroom, in **R Papa** (ed) *Handbook on promoting social justice in education.* Cham: Springer. https://doi.org/10.1007/978-3-030-14625-2_19

McDonagh, J and **McDonagh, S** (1999) Learning to talk, talking to learn, in **J Marsh** and **E Hallett** (eds) *Desirable literacies.* London: Paul Chapman.

McDonald, D, Proctor, P, Gill, W, Heaven, S, Marr, J and **Young, J** (2015) Increasing early childhood educators' use of communication-facilitating and language-modelling strategies: brief speech and language therapy training. *Child Language Teaching and Therapy,* 31 (3): 305–22.

McDonald, D and **Young, J N D** Case study: delivering quality services through growing the evidence base – Nottinghamshire children and families Partnership speech and language therapy service. *Nottinghamshire Healthcare NHS Foundation Trust. RCSLT.* Available at http://sure-start-case-study-nottinghamshire.pdf/

McGilchrist, I (2009) *The master and his emissary: the divided brain and the making of the western world.* London: Yale University Press.

McKean, C, Law, J, Laing, K, Cockerill, M, Allon-Smith, J, McCartney, E. and **Forbes, J** (2017) A qualitative case study in the social capital of co-professional collaborative co-practice for children with speech, language and communication needs. *International Journal of Language & Communication Disorders,* 52 (4): 514–27.

McKean, C, Watson, R, Charlton, J, Roulstone, S, Holme, C, Gilroy, V and **Law, J** (2022) 'Making the most of together time': development of a Health Visitor–led intervention to support children's early language and communication development at the 2–2½-year-old review. *Pilot and Feasibility Studies,* 8 (1): 35.

Mcleod, N (2011) Exploring early years educators' ownership of language and communication knowledge and skills: a review of key policy and initial reflections on every child a talker and its implementation. *International Journal of Primary, Elementary and Early Years Education,* 39 (4): 429–45.

Melhuish, E, et al (2015) *A review of research on the effects of early childhood education and care (ECEC) on children development.* Available at: https://ecec-care.org/resources/publications/. Accessed 9 June 2024

Mercer, N. and **Hodgkinson, S** (eds) (2008) *Exploring talk in school.* London: Sage.

Miller, D (2007) The seeds of learning: young children develop important skills through their gardening activities at a midwestern early education program. *Applied Environmental Education and Communication,* 6 (1): 49–66. https://doi.org/10.1080/15330150701318828

Ministry of Education (2017) *Te Whariki: early childhood curriculum.* New Zealand: Ministry of Education. Available at: https://www.education.govt.nz/assets/Documents/Early-Childhood/ELS-Te-Whariki-Early-Childhood-Curriculum-ENG-Web.pdf. Accessed 12 July 2023.

Moffatt, L (2016) Start with a seedling: uncovering the kindergarten language and literacy curriculum one leaf at a time. *Language & Literacy (Kingston, Ont),* 18 (3): 89–105. https://doi.org/10. 20360/G2RC84

Money, D (1997) A comparison of three approaches to delivering a speech and language therapy service to people with learning disabilities. *International Journal of Language & Communication Disorders*, 32 (4): 449–66.

Montgomery, H and **Cooper, V** (2019) Chapter 4. I blame the parents: families, experts and the state. In *Critical practice with children and young People* (2nd edn.) edited by **Robb, M** and **Thomson, R.** UK: The Policy Press.

Morgan, L, **Marshall, J**, **Harding, S**, **Powell, G**, **Wren, Y**, **Coad, J** and **Roulstone, S** (2019) 'It depends': characterizing speech and language therapy for preschool children with developmental speech and language disorders. *International Journal of Language & Communication Disorders*, 54 (6): 954–970.

Morgan, S and **Dipper, L** (2018) Is the communication pyramid a useful model of language development? *RCSLT Bulletin article*. 26–28.

Morris, K (2018) Executive functions: skills that underpin success. In **P Preedy**, **K Sanderson** and **C Ball** (eds) *Early childhood education redefined: reflections and recommendations on the impact of start right*. London: Routledge.

Murcia, M, **Campbell, C** and **Aranda, G** (2018) Trends in early childhood education practice and professional learning with digital technologies, *Pedagogika* 68 (3): 249–64.

Murray, A and **Egan, S** (2014) Does reading to infants benefit their cognitive development at 9-months-old? An investigation using a large birth cohort survey. *Child Language Teaching and Therapy*, 30 (3): 303–15.

Murray, L and **Andrews, A** (2005) *The social baby*. Richmond: The Children's Project.

Mustonen, R, **Torppa, R** and **Stolt, S** (2022) Screen time of preschool-aged children and their mothers, and children's language development. *Children*, 9 (10): 1577. https://doi.org/10.3390/children9101577

NCCA (2009) *Aistear: the early childhood curriculum framework*. Dublin: NCCA

Neaum, S (2012) *Language and literacy for the early years*. London: Learning Matters.

Nelson, H D, **Nygren, P**, **Walker, M** and **Panoscha, R** (2006) Screening for speech and language delay in preschool children: systematic evidence review for the US preventive services task force. *Pediatrics*, 117 (2): e298–e319.

Neumann, M. M. (2014) An examination of touch screen tablets and emergent literacy in Australian pre-school children. *Australian Journal of Education*, 58 (2): 109–22.

NHS England (2024) *Communities of practice*. Available at: https://library.hee.nhs.uk/knowledge-mobilisation/knowledge-mobilisation-toolkit/communities-of-practice. Accessed 9 June 2024.

Nicholson, N (2020) *Supporting children with identified speech, language and communication needs at two-years-old: voices of early years practitioners*. Post-Doctoral thesis, University of Lincoln.

Nicholson, N and **Palaiologou, I** (2016) Early years foundation stage progress check at the age of two for early intervention in relation to speech and language difficulties in England: the voices of the team around the child. *Early Child Development and Care*, 186 (12): 2009–2021.

Nimmo, J and **Hallett, B** (2008) Childhood in the garden: a place to encounter natural and social diversity, *Young Children*, 63(1): 32–38.

Noddings, N (1984) *Caring, a feminine approach to ethics & moral education*. Berkeley, CA: University of California Press.

Nutbrown, C, **Clough, P**, **Davies, K** and **Hannon, P** (2022) *Home learning environments for young children*. London: SAGE.

Nutbrown, C (2012) *Foundations for quality: The independent review of early education and childcare qualifications.* UK: HMSO.

Office of Health Improvement and Disparities (2024) *Fingertips: public health data. Child development: percentage of children achieving the expected level in communication skills at 2 to 2 and a half years.* Available at: https://fingertips.phe.org.uk/profile/child-health-profiles/data#page/4/gid/1938133223/pat/159/par/K02000001/ati/15/are/E92000001/iid/93431/age/241/sex/4/cat/-1/ctp/-1/yrr/1/cid/4/tbm/1. Accessed 9 June 2024.

Ofsted (2016) *Unknown children: destined for disadvantage.* Manchester: HMSO.

Ofsted (2019) *Education Inspection Framework.* https://www.gov.uk/government/publications/education-inspection-framework. Accessed September 6, 2024.

Ofsted (2023) *Best start in life part 1: setting the scene.* Manchester: HMSO. Available at: https://www.gov.uk/government/publications/best-start-in-life-a-research-review-for-early-years/best-start-in-life-part-1-setting-the-scene. Accessed 3 March 2024.

Pacey (2024) *English as an additional language.* https://www.pacey.org.uk/working-in-childcare/spotlight-on/2-year-olds/english-as-an-additional-language/. Accessed September 6, 2024.

Palaiologou, I (2016) Children under five and digital technologies: implications for early years' pedagogy, *European Early Childhood Education Research Journal*, 24 (1): 5–24.

Parveen, N (2019) Funding for pupils with special educational needs drops 17%. *The Guardian*, 3 April. Available at: https://www.theguardian.com/education/2019/apr/04/funding-pupils-special-educational-needs-send-drops-north-england

Paul, R, Murray, C, Clancy, K and **Andrews, D** (1997) Reading and metaphonological outcomes in late talkers. *Journal of Speech, Language, and Hearing Research*, 40 (5): 1037–47.

PHE (2020) *Best start in speech, language and communication: Supporting evidence.* UK: PHE.

Piaget, J (1965) *The moral judgment of the child.* New York: The Free Press. (Original work published 1932).

Pinker, S (1994) *The language instinct.* London: Penguin.

Preece, D and **Zhao, Y**, (2015) Multi-sensory storytelling: a tool for teaching or an intervention technique? *British Journal of Special Education*, 42 (4): 429–43.

Pretty, J, Angus, C, Bain, M, Barton, J, Gladwell, V, Hine, R, Pilgrim, S, Sandercock, G and **Sellens, M** (2009) *Nature, childhood, health and life pathways. Interdisciplinary Centre for Environment and Society Occasional Paper 2009-02*: University of Essex.

Prout, A (2005) *The future of childhood.* London: Taylor Francis.

Public Health England (2020) *Best start in speech, language and communication: Guidance to support local commissioners and service leads.* Available at: https://www.gov.uk/government/publications/best-start-in-speech-language-and-communication. Accessed 9 June 2024.

Raschle, N M, Becker, B L C, Smith, S, Fehlbaum, L V, Wang, Y and **Gaab, N** (2015) Investigating the influences of language delay and/or familial risk for dyslexia on brain structure in 5-year-olds. *Cerebral Cortex*, 27 (1): 764–76.

Reed, M (2012) What do we mean by quality and quality improvement? In **M Reed** and **N Canning** (eds) *Implementing quality improvement and change in the early years.* London: Sage Publications.

Richardson, T (2014) *Speech and language development in a forest school environment: an action research project.* London: SAGE Research Methods Cases. Available at: http://srmo.sagepub.com/view/methods-case-studies-2013/n342.xml

Richardson, T and **Murray, J** (2016) Are young children's utterances affected by characteristics of their learning environments? A multiple case study. *Early Child Development and Care*, 187 (3–4): 457–68.

Richardson, T, Waite, S, Askerlund, P, Almers, E and **Hvit-Lindstrand, S** (2023) How does nature support early language learning? A systematic literature review. *Early Years*. https://doi.org/10.1080/09575146.2023.2220978

Roberts, R (2002) *Self esteem and successful early learning* (2nd edn.). London: Hodder & Stoughton.

Robinson, M and **Cottrell, D** (2005) Health professionals in multi-disciplinary and multi-agency teams: changing professional practice. *Journal of Interprofessional Care*, 19 (6): 547–60.

Rovira, LC (2008) The relationship between language and identity. The use of the home language as a human right of the immigrant. *REMHU-Revista Interdisciplinar da Mobilidade Humana*, 16(31), 63–81.

Rowland, C (2013) *Understanding child language acquisition*. London: Routledge.

Royal College of Speech and Language Therapists (2017) *England SEND reforms 2017* Available at: https://www.rcslt.org/-/media/Project/RCSLT/send-report-jan2017.pdf

Royal College of Speech and Language Therapists (2021) *Curriculum guidance for the pre-registration education of speech and language therapists*. Available at: https://www.rcslt.org/wp-content/uploads/2020/08/RCSLT-Curriculum-Guidance-March2021.pdf. Accessed 9 June 2024.

Royal College of Speech and Language Therapists (2024) *We are the village: speech language and communication in the early years*. Available at: https://www.rcslt.org/wp-content/uploads/2024/04/Early-years_We-are-the-Village-report_NI_April-2024.pdf. Accessed 9 June 2024.

Royal College of Speech and Language Therapists (N.D) *What are speech, language and communication needs?* Available at https://www.rcslt.org/-/media/Project/RCSLT/send-report-jan2017.pdf

Sakr, M and **Bonetti, S** (2021) Continuing professional development for the early years workforce in England since 2015: a synthesis of survey data highlighting commonalities, discrepancies and gaps. *Early Years*, 43 (2): 395–410.

Saxton, M (2017) *Child language: acquisition and development* (2nd edn.). London: Sage Publications.

Scottish Government (2016) *Ready to Act – A transformational plan for Children and young people, their parents, carers and families who require support from allied health professionals*. Available at: https://www.gov.scot/publications/ready-act-transformational-plan-children-young-people-parents-carers-families/. Accessed 9 June 2024.

Scottish Government (2020) *Realising the ambition: Being Me. National practice guidance for early years in Scotland*. Available at: https://education.gov.scot/media/3bjpr3wa/realisingtheambition.pdf. Accessed 9 June 2024.

Scottish Government (2009) *The early years framework*. Scotland: Directorate of children and families.

Scott-Phillips, T (2015) *Speaking our minds: why human communication is different, and how language evolved to make it special*. Basingstoke: Palgrave Macmillan.

Siraj-Blatchford, I and **Clarke, P** (2000) *Supporting identity, diversity, and language in the early years*. Maidenhead; New York: Open University Press.

Siraj-Blatchford, I, Sylva, K, Muttock, S, Gilden, R, and **Bell, D** (2002). *Researching Effective Pedagogy in the Early Years (REPEY) DfES Research Report 365*. HMSO London: Queen's Printer.

Skinner, B (1957) *Verbal behaviour*. New York: Appleton-Century-Crofts.

Skinner, E A, Kindermann, T and **Mashburn, A** (2019) *Lifespan developmental systems.* London: Routledge.

Slade, M, Lowery, C and **Bland, K** (2013) Evaluating the impact of forest schools: a collaboration between a university and a primary school. *British Journal of Learning Support* 28 (2): 66–72.

Snow, C E and **Matthews, T J** (2016) Reading and language in the early grades, *The Future of Children*, 26 (2), 57–74.

Sood, K, and **Mistry, M T** (2011) English as an additional language: is there a need to embed cultural values and beliefs in institutional practice? *Education 3-13*, 39 (2): 203–15. https://doi.org/10.1080/03004270903389913. Accessed 13 May 2024.

Soomro, N and **Soomro, S**, (2018) Autism children's app using PECS. *Annals of Emerging Technologies in Computing (AETiC)*, 2 (1): 7–16.

Standards Testing Agency (2015) *2016 assessment and reporting arrangements: PDF format versions.* GOV. UK.https://www.gov.uk/government/publications/2016-assessment-and-reporting-arrangements-pdf-format-versions

Stewart, K and **Waldfogel, J.** (2017) *Closing gaps early.* UK: The Sutton Trust.

Streelasky, J (2019) A forest-based environment as a site of literacy and meaning making for kindergarten children. *Literacy* 53 (2): 95–101. https://doi.org/10.1111/lit.12155

Strong-Wilson, T and **Ellis, J** (2007) Children and place: Reggio Emilia's environment as third teacher. *Theory Into Practice*, 46 (1): 40–47.

Sudrajat, D (2017) Language development and acquisition in childhood stage: psycholinguistic review. *Intelegensia: Jurnal Pendidikan dan.*

Sutterby, J and **Frost, J** (2006) Creating play environments for early childhood: indoors and out. In **B Spodek** and **O Saracho** (eds) *Handbook of research on the education of young children* (2nd edn). Mahwah NJ: Lawrence Erlbaum Associates.

Sylva, K and **Eisenstadt, N** (2024) *Transforming early childhood: narrowing the gap between children from lower- and higher-income families.* Available at: https://www.nesta.org.uk/report/transforming-early-childhood-narrowing-the-gap-between-children-from-lower-and-higher-income-families/. Accessed 9 June 2024.

Sylva, K (2010) *Early childhood matters: evidence from the effective pre-school and primary education project.* Abingdon, Oxon: Routledge.

Sylva, K, Melhuish, E, Sammons, P, Siraj-Blatchford, I and **Taggart, B** (2004) *The effective provision of pre-School education (EPPE) project: Final report: a longitudinal study funded by the DfES 1997-2004.* Nottingham: DfES Publications.

Talbot, D (2024) *Languages spoken in UK – WordsRated.* Wordsrated. Available at: https://wordsrated.com/languages-spoken-in-uk. Accessed 14 May 2024.

Tamis-LeMonda, C, Bornstein, M and **Baumwell, L** (2001) Maternal responsiveness and children's achievement of language milestones. *Child Development.* 72 (3): 748–767.

Tan, C T, Johnston, A, Ballard, K, Ferguson, S and **Perera-Schulz, D** (2013) SPeAK-MAN: towards popular gameplay for speech therapy. In *Proceedings of the 9th Australasian Conference on interactive Entertainment: Matters of Life and Death (IE '13).* Association for Computing Machinery, 28, 1–4.

The British Society for Early Education. Available at: https://early-education.org.uk/cultural-capital/. Accessed 25 April 2024.

The Communication Friendly Spaces Approach. Available at: https://www.elizabethjarman.com/

The Communication Trust (2017a) *Professional development in speech, language and communication: Findings from a national survey*. Available at: https://www.rcslt.org/wp-content/uploads/media/Project/RCSLT/1tctworkforce-development-report-final-online.pdf. Accessed 9 June 2024

The Communication Trust (2017b) *Speech Language Communication Framework* Available at: https://www.slcframework.org.uk/. Accessed 27 June 2024.

The Sutton Trust (2024). *CECIL: Final Report Coaching early conversations, interaction and language*. London: The Sutton Trust.

The New Yorker (2021). Forgetting my first language. Available at: https://www.newyorker.com/culture/personal-history/forgetting-my-first-language. Accessed 13 May 2024.

The New Zealand Ministry of Education (2017) *Te Whariki: Early Childhood Curriculum*. http://els-te-whariki-early-childhood-curriculum-eng-web.pdf/. Accessed 30 April 2024.

Tickell, C (2011) *The early years: foundations for life, health and learning*. UK: Crown copyright.

Tizard, B and **Hughes, M** (1984) *Young children learning, talking and thinking at home*. London: Fontana Books.

Together towards inclusion TOOLKIT FOR DIVERSITY IN THE PRIMARY SCHOOL. (n.d.) Available at: https://ncca.ie/media/2030/assessment toolkit.pdf. Accessed 2 April 2024.

Tomasello, M (2003) *Constructing language: a usage-based theory of language acquisition*. London: Harvard University Press.

Trevarthen, C (2002) Learning in companionship. *Education in the North: The Journal of Scottish Education, New Series*, 10, 16–25. The University of Aberdeen, Faculty of Education.

Trevarthen, C (1978) Communication and cooperation in early infancy: a description of primary intersubjectivity. Chapter in Bullowa, M. *Before speech: the Beginning of Interpersonal Communication*.

Tudge, J R H, Navarro, J L, Merçon-Vargas, E A and **Payir, A** (2021) The promise and the practice of early childhood educare in the writings of Urie Bronfenbrenner. *Early Child Development and Care*. 191 (7–8): 1079–88.

Tura, F, Wood, C, Lushey, C, Paechter, C and **Wood, J** (2020) *Evaluation of small steps big changes: interim report*. Nottingham: Nottingham Centre for Children, Young People and Families.

UK Government (2024). *Family Hubs*. https://familyhubs.campaign.gov.uk/. Accessed 9/6/24.

Vallotton, C and **Ayoub, C** (2011) Use your words. *Early Childhood Research Quarterly*, 26 (2): 169–81.

van der Westhuizen, L M and **Hannaway, D M** (2021) Digital play for language development in the early grades, *South African Journal of Childhood Education*, 11 (1): a925.

Vesty, S and **Wardle, L** (2014) Exploring children's wellbeing and motivations. In **A Woods** (ed) *The characteristics of effective learning creating and capturing the possibilities in the early years*. London: Taylor & Francis Ltd.

Vidal-Hall, C, Flewitt, R and **Wyse, D** (2020) Early childhood practitioner beliefs about digital media: integrating technology into a child-centred classroom environment. *European Early Childhood Education Research Journal*, 28 (2): 167–81.

Vygotsky, L (1962) *Thought and language*. Cambridge: MIT Press.

Vygotsky, L S (1978) *Mind in society: the development of higher psychological processes*. London: Harvard University Press.

Waite, S and **Pratt, N** (2013) Theoretical perspectives on learning outside the classroom: relationships between learning and place. In **S Waite** (ed) *Children learning outside the classroom: from birth to eleven.* London: Sage Publications.

Wall, K (2011) *Special needs and early years a practitioner's guide* (3rd edn). London: SAGE.

Warren, K, Franklin, C and **Streeter, K**. (1998) New directions in systems theory: Chaos and complexity. *Social Work*, 43(4): 357–72.

Wellings, E (2012) *Forest school national governing body business plan 2012.* Cumbria: Institute for outdoor learning.

Welsh Government (2024) *Flying start programme.* https://www.gov.wales/flying-start-programme. Accessed 9 June 2024

Welsh Government (2020) *Talk with me: Speech, Language and Communication (SLC) delivery plan.* Cardiff: Welsh Government.

West, M, Boshoff, K and **Stewart, H** (2016) A qualitative exploration of the characteristics and practices of interdisciplinary collaboration. *South African Journal of Occupational Therapy*, 46(3): 27–34.

Whalley, M (2006) 'Leadership in integrated centres and services for children and families – a community development approach: engaging with the struggle', children's issues, *Journal of the Children's Issues Centre*, 10 (2): 8.

Whalley, M (ed) (1997) *Working with parents.* Sevenoaks: Hodder and Soughton.

Whitebread, D, Kuvalja, M and **O'Connor, A** (2015) Quality in early childhood education: an international review and guide for policy makers. *Report for the World Innovation Summit for Education.* Dohar: WISE.

Wilson, R (2018) *Nature and young children; encouraging creative play and learning in natural environments.* London: Routledge.

Winsler, K, Midgley, K J, Grainger, J and **Holcomb, P J** (2018) An electrophysiological megastudy of spoken word recognition. *Language, Cognition and Neuroscience*, 33(8): 1063–82.

Yoon, HS, Templeton, TN (2019) The practice of listening to children: the challenges of hearing children out in an adult-regulated world. *Harvard Educational Review*, 89 (1): 55–84. https://doi.org/10.17763/1943-5045-89.1.55

INDEX

Zeitfracht Medien GmbH
Ferdinand-Jühlke-Straße 7
99095 Erfurt, Deutschland
produktsicherheit@kolibri360.de